MANAGING INTERCULTURAL NEGOTIATIONS

*Guidelines for Trainers
and Negotiators*

Pierre Casse
and
Surinder Deol

First Edition

INTERNATIONAL

The International Society for Intercultural Education, Training and Research

Washington, DC

Published by:

SIETAR International
1414 Twenty-Second St. N.W.
Washington, D.C. 20037
(202) 296-4710

First Edition
February 1985

Library of Congress Catalog Card Number: 84-72589
ISBN 0-933934-11-4

Manufactured in the United States of America

10 9 8 7 6 5 4 3 2 1

Dedicated to René Springuel and Orlando Peña,
two friends from opposite sides of the world

Table of Contents

"Man does not know himself, he does not know anything, yet he has theories about everything. Most of these theories are lying."

P.D. Ouspensky

". . . Most of our lies will work out really well if you act as if they are true."

R. Bandler and J. Grinder

Acknowledgements

The authors wish to express their gratitude for permission to use the following materials:

R. Bandler and J. Grinder for material regarding hypnosis and negotiation found on pages 118-119 from *Frogs into Princes,* 1979. Used with permission of Real People Press.

R. Fisher and W. Ury for the use of their chart on page 93 concerning the three approaches to negotiation, taken from *Getting to Yes,* copyright 1981 by the Houghton Mifflin Company, Boston, MA.

The Huthwaite Research Group for the use of "The Behavior of Successful Negotiators," 1976 found on pages 23-24.

O. Ichazo for material found on pages 130-131 from *The Human Process of Enlightenment and Freedom,* copyright 1976, published in New York by Arica.

C. L. Karrass for information found on pages 22-23 from *The Negotiating Game,* pp. 15-26, copyright 1970 by Thomas Y. Crowell Co. Reprinted by permission of Harper & Row, Publishers, Inc.

For the Self-Assessment Exercise on Listening Skills on pages 43-44 by R. T. Moran and R. P. Harris, from *Managing Cultural Synergy,* pp. 88-89, copyright 1982. Used with permission of the Gulf Publishing Company in Houston, Texas.

P. D. Ouspensky for the definition of intercultural negotiation which is found on page xiii, from *The Fourth Way,* page 23, copyright 1971 by Vintage Books in New York.

The Art of Japanese Management by R. T. Pascale and A. G. Athos for material found on pages 45-46. Used with permission of Simon & Schuster, Inc., copyright 1981.

R. Patai for his description of an Arab negotiator found on pages 150-151, from *The Arab Mind,* copyright 1973 by Charles Scribner & Sons, New York.

"Conflict-resolution Strategies" by J. A. Stepsis, found on pages 50-52, from *The 1974 Annual Handbook for Group Facilitators,* pp 139-141. Edited by J. W. Pfeiffer and J. E. Jones. Used with permission of University Associates.

Materials found on pages 72-75, from *A Handbook of Structured Experiences for Human Relations Training, Volume III,* edited by J. W. Pfeiffer and J. E. Jones. Copyright 1974. Used with permission of University Associates.

The pictures found on page 107-109 taken by N. S. Lybrand, from "Gestures: Perceptions and Response," *The 1981 Annual Handbook for Group Facilitators,* pages 28-33, edited by J. W. Pfeiffer and J. E. Jones. Used with permission of University Associates.

"Understanding Communication Effectiveness" by G. J. Rath and K. S. Stoyanoff, found on page 114, from *The 1982 Annual for Facilitators, Trainers and Consultants,* page 166, edited by J. W. Pfeiffer and L.D. Goodstein. Used with permission of University Associates.

J. Phillips-Martinsson for the portrait of a Swedish negotiator found on page 151, from *Swedes as Others See Them,* copyright 1982 by Utbildringshuset/Studentlitteratur in Lund, Sweden.

Selected American characteristics by V. Lynn Tyler found on pages 136-137, from *Reading Between the Lines,* copyright 1978 by the Eyring Research Institute.

The authors also wish to acknowledge with gratitude M. L. Bussat for providing the cover photograph; Marcia Smith and Judy Verbits for their editorial assistance and patience in seeing this book to completion; and Dr. Diane L. Zeller for her encouragement and for managing this project with her usual efficiency and enthusiasm.

Preface

Purpose of the Book

In this book (which is more of a self-workbook than anything else), we have tried to use the Zen approach, which is to point with our fingers and say to the readers, "Look here, look there, it seems there is something interesting and useful."

One word of caution. Please do look here and there, not at our fingers which are only instruments of our curious minds.

Format of the Book

The reader is invited to experience ten workshops that provide group exercises, simulations, self-assessment exercises, critical incidents, role-playing, and mini case studies. The workshops cover a selection of critical issues related to negotiation, i.e., how to: define the importance of negotiation in our day-to-day life, be a successful negotiator, plan and prepare oneself for negotiations, improve our negotiating skills and styles, select the right negotiation strategies and tactics, use non-verbal communication to one's advantage, explore the Gestalt approach to negotiation, and finally, negotiate across cultures. So the book is basically a "how to" instrument. That is why we have used the workshop approach to present our materials in a highly practical way. An identical format has been used for each workshop that includes:

1. A brief introduction to the topic or issue;
2. A description of the aim;
3. A presentation of the objectives;
4. Three exercises and their related conceptual frameworks;
5. An estimate of the time needed to run the workshop;
6. A list of supplementary readings.

Some of the materials have already been presented in two other SIETAR publications.[1] However, we have reviewed and explored them in a completely new way.

Guidelines on the Use of the Book

The book, which is meant for trainers and negotiators, should be read in a creative frame of mind. We don't claim to present absolute truth, as perfect evidence of what successful negotiation is. Not at all. We just want to draw the attention of those who are interested in negotiation to some of the clues that we have collected during our international and intercultural experiences. People who approach the field for the first time could select the topics

---

[1]Casse, P. *Training for the Cross-Cultural Mind.* Washington, D.C.: SIETAR, 1980. Casse, P. *Training for the Multicultural Manager.* Washington, D.C.: SIETAR, 1982.

and exercises that are simple and to the point. We suggest that they concentrate first on defining intercultural negotiations; the profile of a successful intercultural negotiator; and negotiation skills, types, and styles. More advanced trainers could right away organize workshops around pre-negotiation planning, negotiation strategies and tactics, non-verbal communication, and negotiation. Professional trainers could not only deal with more complex issues such as a Gestalt approach to negotiation or the use of hypnosis in negotiation, but also create their own training materials on the basis of the ones presented in the book.

Keep in mind that the exercises do not lead to the establishment of universal rules or principles (if such things exist) but to the discovery of what is good and effective for one person at a certain time in a defined situation. Again we want to stress the importance of learning how to learn in this field as in others.

So trainers should use the book in a cautious, exploratory way. Ideally, we believe that each reader involved in training could design and implement the ten workshops so that they end up writing their own book on negotiation.

One Last Word

We are fully aware of the fact that our style may seem "strange," our quotations esoteric, and the exercises ambiguous, if not inconclusive.

Our style is indeed strange. It is a style created by two persons (shall we say "individual cultures") who met and created through the synergistic process a unique way to present ideas to others. Is the style good or bad? We don't think that it really matters. The key question is whether the style prevents the reader from learning or if, on the contrary, it helps them enhance their awareness and skills. It is, of course, up to the users of the book to decide.

Our quotations are esoteric on purpose. They aim at involving the readers at their unconscious level. They can thus read them and just move on without spending too much time on their meanings. They should not worry if they look obscure, unrelated to the text that follows — their unconscious minds will understand. In their own way, of course, that's what we believe.

Regarding the ambiguity of some of the exercises, the explanation is quite simple: we did our best to eliminate the obscurities related to the presentation of the exercise objectives, processes, and outputs. We do realize that we have not been completely successful, but honestly, is it so critical? Can't we for once use the Japanese approach and exploit the same ambiguity to be more flexible, creative and effective? Why not? Again, the readers (or the "market" as the Americans say) will judge.

If we have been successful in introducing (negotiating) the book, at least some people will read it, use it, and who knows, enjoy it!

Introduction

"The human biocomputer is constantly being programmed,
continually, simply and naturally, below its levels of awareness,
by the surrounding environment."

J.C. Lilly

The formal purpose of this book is to address three issues namely: Why do we negotiate? What is intercultural negotiation? How do we negotiate and improve what we are already doing well?

The informal intention (the hidden agenda?) of this introduction to the management of negotiations is to persuade as many readers as possible to accept that negotiation is indeed what we do all the time; that there are practical ways to enhance our effectiveness as negotiators; and finally, the world desperately needs "good" negotiators.

As a matter of fact, we claim that we have no choice but to improve our capability to control our psychological, cultural, and natural realities so that we survive and move ahead as a species. That is what negotiation is about. Nothing more. Nothing less.

Let's remember one of our first negotiations. A long time ago (not that long really), some human beings discovered fire. Terrified by the power of their discovery, they got used to it after a while, and thrilled by the apparently unlimited potential of that mysterious source of light and heat, they started to go around to share with mankind the benefits of fire. To their amazement, they mainly got three types of reactions: anger and hostility (We do not want that "new" thing!), indifference and passivity (Why should we bother?), and interest and envy (How come you got it and not us?).

This could be the story of human life. Let us thus negotiate.

Why Negotiation?

"What is fate?" Nasrudin was asked by a scholar.
"An endless succession of intertwined events, each influencing the other."
"That is hardly a satisfactory answer. I believe in cause and effect."
"Very well," said the Mulla, "Look at that." He pointed to a procession passing in the street.
"The man is being taken to be hanged. Is that because someone gave him a silver piece and enabled him to buy the knife with which he committed the murder; or because someone saw him do it; or because nobody stopped him?"

I. Shah

We negotiate all the time or, to put it differently, human beings are in a constant state of negotiation. We negotiate with others. We negotiate with nature. It is an ongoing process. It is crucial for our survival. It is life.

Since it seems that we always want more and better (for good or bad), we have to behave so that we are able to influence our environment (including people) to move toward our goals.

The problem is that everything and everybody resists our attempts to change what is at a certain point in time. We have therefore to convince ourselves and others that it is in the interests of all to alter a temporary state of equilibrium.

We negotiate with ourselves in the sense that we have to mediate between our conflicting values, convictions, feelings, perceptions, and assumptions to remain alive, be sane, and grow with a minimum of pain.

We negotiate with others and try to get them to change (or not to change) their behavior because it is in our and their best interest.

We negotiate with all the existing systems that are part of our social and natural environments. We must negotiate with them to avoid being crushed, destroyed, or alienated by the invisible forces that surround our species as well as by the uncontrolled cultural products of our social associations.

So we have no choice. We must find our way around, push, pull, change things, adapt, be, and become without disrupting (too much) that very delicate internal and external balance of our world.

That is apparently why we negotiate. We have no choice. Do we?

What is Intercultural Negotiation?

> *"Fishes, asking what water was, went to a wise fish.*
> *He told them that it was all around them, yet they still thought*
> *that they were thirsty."*
>
> I. Shah

Before defining intercultural negotiation, we would like to examine three premises which, we believe, have a tremendous impact on the types of negotiation we get involved in.

Firstly, we are still alive because we got (nobody knows how, from where, or from whom for that matter) the power to create cultures. The human psyche, yours and ours, has the ability to create symbols as well as meanings out of nothing. We still exist because we make sense of what is, without actually knowing what "is" is. Cultures are paradigms for human survival.

Secondly, we live in a world made up of our own subjective constructions. These constructions are fictions in the sense that they do not actually reflect reality nor explain it. The amazing phenomenon is that those fictions, which only exist in our minds, enable us to live together, and cope with nature. In other words, they work.

Thirdly, each individual has a unique way to look at the world and create it. Each of us is a culture in himself or herself. We have been biologically programmed to create, to produce cultures in many various ways.

From the above considerations, we can deduce that all human interactions are, by definition, intercultural. When two individuals meet, it is an intercultural encounter since they both have different (sometimes drastically different, if not opposite) ways to perceive, discover, create reality.

All negotiations are therefore intercultural. Negotiations with a boss, spouse, child, friend, fellow employee, union representative, official from a foreign country, and so on are all interculturally loaded.

Even the internal negotiating process related to decision making (shall I do it or not? talk or not? express feelings or not?) is intercultural since it involves at least two different perceptions of the self and its relationship with the outside world. The conscious mind does not construct the world the same way that the unconscious does. As a matter of fact, "we" are always at the center of a powerful negotiating play between the forces of the culturally programmed conscious mind and the unconstricted thrusts of the culturally free subconscious or unconscious mind. As C. G. Jung stated ". . . the life of the individual is not determined solely by the gap and its opinions or by social factors, but quite as much, if not more, by a transcendent authority."

Intercultural negotiations do not only exist because people who think, feel, and behave differently have to reach agreements on practical matters such as how to produce, consume, organize, and distribute power and grant rewards, but because of the very nature of the challenging, unpredictable, and contradictory world we live in. We are forced to negotiate.

Moreover, we have reached a point where it is becoming more and more important to be aware of and understand the subjective cultural constructions of past and present societies, to integrate them into systems which will enable us to pursue our journey to our unknown destination.[1]

That task certainly requires some kind of negotiation. No less dramatic is the fact that we have apparently reached a point in our evolution where we produce cultural phenomena (values, beliefs, and assumptions) that can be destructive for the entire species. If we want to survive, we must learn how to control our cultural products so that they will not destroy us. It is becoming more and more urgent to "manage" our cultural constructions as well as the spontaneous interactions between them.

---

[1]"We must remember that man is created in a very interesting way by nature. He is developed up to a certain point; after this point he must develop himself. Nature does not develop man beyond a certain point." (Ouspensky, P.D. *The Fourth Way,* New York: Vintage Books, 1971, pg. 23.)

That also implies the use of negotiation, doesn't it? Finally, at the risk of shocking the reader, we go as far as to say that we have the feeling that to achieve the above — awareness and control — we shall have to go through some genetic changes. And we do not think that this is negotiable!

How Do We Negotiate?

> *A man saw Nasrudin searching for something on the ground.*
> *"What have you lost, Mulla?" he asked.*
> *"My key," said the Mulla.*
> *So the man went down on his knees too, and they both looked for it. After a time, the other man asked: "Where exactly did you drop it?"*
> *"In my house."*
> *"Then why are you looking here?"*
> *"There is more light here than inside my own house."*
>
> I. Shah

There are many cultural ways to approach negotiation. For some people negotiation is a game with winners and losers; for others it is a serious matter, a joint venture to find fair and effective solutions to existing problems; a necessity of life with not too many choices around.

Some negotiators prepare themselves thoroughly before the negotiating encounters; others trust their intuition and are ready to adapt to the negotiation according to its dynamics. Many assumptions influence the negotiation process. Here are some of our own assumptions:

1. *What is in my mind is also in yours — potentially*
   The implication of this assumption is that I can be you and you can be me: We can indeed understand each other and we can also learn from each other through the actualization of you in me and me in you.

2. *What I shall think, believe, and do tomorrow is already in my mind — potentially*
   This basically means that everybody's actions are, in a way, predetermined (with options): The more expanded my mind, the more options I shall have tomorrow: What we become is what we are.

3. *All human life patterns exist in any individual mind — potentially*
   This assumption implies that we can become everything culturally speaking: Our unconscious mind is free to actualize all kinds of cultural patterns: To be culturally flexible is the key to survival in tomorrow's world.

We strongly believe that intercultural negotiators should keep in mind that when they talk about "them" they are actually talking about themselves (we are also them); that when they criticize a certain way to think, feel, and behave that they dislike in others, they are in fact making a cultural projection and in so doing, expressing a cultural trait that they own too, but which is underdeveloped or not yet actualized within their own cross-cultural minds; that when they analyze cultures, they stereotype and use over-generalizations (which is acceptable as long as they know that they are doing it and control the process); that the absolute cultural truth does not exist, or rather, it exists under various expressions or forms according to the constraints of the time and space they are in.

We realize that we have not answered the question: how do we negotiate? That is exactly what this book claims to cover. It is based on observations of many intercultural negotiations at the local, regional, national and international levels: It tries to discover skills, styles, strategies, and tactics that effective intercultural negotiators tend to use.

Washington, D.C. *Pierre Casse*
September 1984 *Surinder Deol*

"Successful intercultural negotiators are aware that people indeed think, feel, and behave differently and are at the same time, equally logical and rational. They know that individuals, groups, communities, organizations, and nations have different values, beliefs, and assumptions that make sense from their own viewpoints. They are sensitive to the fact that everybody perceives, discovers, and constructs reality — the internal and external world — in various meaningful ways. They are convinced that to be different is good as long as the differences are under control or managed."

Pierre Casse
Surinder Deol

Photograph by M. L. Bussat

CHAPTER 1
Defining Intercultural Negotiation

"In the Japanese language, verbs appear at the ends of sentences, so the listener doesn't know where the speaker is headed until he gets there, the speaker can change his verbs in response to the listener's expression."

R. T. Pascale and A. G. Athos

We live in a world where we negotiate all the time without ourselves being aware of it. Whenever we want or need to gain something that is not under our control, we negotiate and try to reach an agreement that gives us access to or use of that precious something. The process may be extremely painful at times, depending on the positions taken by our "opponents." If we are faced with a hard negotiator we need to organize our resources carefullly and select appropriate strategies and tactics in a conscious manner so that our objective is achieved. This however, does not mean that *negotiation is winning all the time.* Any purposeful and mutually fruitful negotiation assumes a win-win situation in which both parties gain something, though the gains are rarely proportionate. This win-win assumption is critical in the cross-cultural field as win-lose negotiations tend to be wasteful exercises, resulting in bitterness and hard feelings amongst groups of people who could have otherwise enjoyed healthy and progressive business relations. We believe that: (a) it is possible to understand and manage processes underlying cross-cultural negotiations; (b) the knowledge of negotiating skills, types, styles, and modes is critical and this can be acquired through sharing experiences with others; and (c) more skilful and successful negotiators have personality characteristics that distinguish them from those who are less effective as negotiators. *We can learn to be effective cross-cultural negotiators.*

Workshop 1

1. Aim: To help participants understand the meaning and implications of intercultural negotiation.

2. Objectives: Participants will:

(1) Define international and intercultural negotiations;

(2) Analyze some of their assumptions regarding negotiations;

(3) Examine the process of managing negotiations.

3. Process:

First Exercise. The trainer introduces the concept of intercultural negotiation. The discussion centers around the theme that *we negotiate all the time.* The growth of multinational business during the last three decades, interdependence amongst developing and developed economies, transfer of technologies and technical skills (North-South and South-South), advances in communications, increase in cross-national tourism, and the development of infrastructural support systems to sustain international exchanges are some of the important factors that have underscored the need for frequent international exchanges between businesspeople, professionals, researchers, trainers, scientists, diplomats, journalists, government officials, and officials of international agencies.

More often we come across people from different cultures who have other sets of assumptions and subscribe to value systems sometimes radically opposed to our own. How do we interact with them to transact any meaningful business or build mutually beneficial contacts aimed at satisfying our needs? In these and similar situations, our negotiating abilities or skills prove invaluable. Success in negotiations across cultures thus implies understanding and appreciation of varied cultural systems in which others are placed and reinforcement of skills that enhance our effectiveness in such cross-cultural transactions.

Negotiation from this perspective is the *process by which at least two parties with different cultural values, beliefs, needs, and viewpoints try to reach agreement on a matter of mutual interest.* This definition implies that: (a) the parties involved belong to different cultures and therefore do not share the same ways of thinking, feeling, and behaving or the same values, beliefs, and assumptions; (b) the negotiation takes place in a cross-cultural environment, e.g., an international organization, third party culture; and (c) the matter at stake is of cross-cultural interest. The trainer presents this definition and the group is asked to explore (evaluate, criticize, expand) these implications in light of its collective as well as individual intercultural experiences.

Second Exercise. The trainer asks the participants to evolve their own definition of intercultural negotiation. For this purpose, small groups of five or six participants are formed. The process goes like this:

Step 1. Each participant is asked to complete the sentence: "Negotiation is . . ." (5 minutes).

Step 2. Participants meet in small groups and share their definitions of negotiation. This is a brainstorming exercise where free flow of ideas in a non-judgmental atmosphere is encouraged (approximately 10 minutes).

Step 3. Participants select three definitions from the original list. They *negotiate* to arrive at a commonly agreed list (10 minutes).

Step 4. For every definition selected in the final list, participants think about its cross-cultural implications. (15 minutes).

Step 5. Participants meet for debriefing. The trainer asks each group to present one definition of negotiation along with its cross-cultural implications. The group may evolve one comprehensive definition for use during the workshop.

Feedback: Typical reactions of participants in some of our international workshops are summarized below:

Negotiation is . . .	Intercultural implications
• a situation.	• appreciation of cultural differences is essential in cross-cultural situations
• mutual understanding.	• a conscious endeavour to manage cultural differences is required
• communication.	• both parties must be in a position to communicate clearly and overcome cultural barriers to effective communication
• need satisfaction.	• ascertain expectations and then work for their achievement
• compromise or settlement.	• narrow down differences and emphasize commonalities of interest
• a deal.	• both written and unwritten aspects of negotiation are important
• a bargaining process.	• be prepared to give and take
• anticipation.	• familiarize yourself with management styles and assumptions of others to anticipate their moves
	(continued)

Negotiation is . . .	Intercultural implications
• persuasion.	• establish your credibility and be soft while not losing your grip on the problem
• achieving consensus.	• reduce differences to reach an agreement
• practicing empathy.	• appreciate problems and limitations of your "opponents"
• searching for alternatives.	• be systematic and simple (don't try to impress others with complex models)
• conflict management.	• it is possible to manage conflicting interests
• winning.	• it can create problems and generate bad feelings
• a means of getting what you want from others.	• it also means giving what others expect of you
• gaining the favor of people from whom you want things.	• it is easier to gain favors while acting in a genuine and rational manner
• managing power and information.	• know in advance the limitations of your power; gain information while managing the process of negotiation
• time and opportunity management.	• timely actions based on opportunity analysis provide the needed edge in highly competitive situations
• more of an art than a science.	• be natural; don't play on others' sensibilities
• selling.	• create the need first
• the least troublesome method of settling disputes.	• the use of intercultural negotiating styles, modes, and skills is important

Third Exercise. The trainees look at the *picture* below and write a brief story about the negotiation between the various people involved. Then they meet in threes and: (a) share their stories; and (b) analyze some of the main cultural characteristics (values, beliefs, assumptions) of their statements.

A plenary session follows the work in threes. A general discussion (see Input 3) can then take place around the significance of managing (controlling) the negotiation process. The trainer explains the significance of managing (controlling) the negotiation process. The point to be emphasized is that *managing* intercultural negotiation requires *knowledge* of what is happening during the negotiating process, *understanding* of the dynamics involved, *prediction* of the outcome of any move made during the negotiation, and *control* of the process through effective decision making.

A discussion of some of the following five questions may prove useful:

1. What should you know about negotiation?

2. What are the main approaches that can be used to better understand negotiation?

3. How can we predict the outcome of a negotiation?

4. How do we make decisions and solve problems in our cultures?

5. How do we evaluate the outcome of negotiations in our cultural settings?

4. Time: Between 3 and 4 hours.

5. Conceptual Framework:

INPUT 1

The Meaning and Nature
of Negotiation

Gerald I. Nierenberg[1] has quoted the following passage from a study by the Committee for the Judiciary of the U.S. Senate, which throws valuable light on what negotiation means to Americans:

> *"To an American, negotiation is the least troublesome method of settling disputes. Negotiations may be exploratory and serve to formulate viewpoints and delineate areas of agreement or convention. Or it may aim at working out practical arrangements. The success of negotiation depends upon whether (a) the issue is negotiable (that is, you can sell your car but not your child); (b) the negotiators interested not only in taking but also in giving are able to exchange value for value, and are willing to compromise; or (c) negotiating parties trust each other to some extent — if they didn't, a plethora of safety provisions would render the 'agreement' unworkable."*

Nierenberg doubts the validity of the three conditions that the Committee suggested as prerequisites to success:

> In some circumstances even children (kidnapping, for instance) are negotiable. "All issues must be considered negotiable whenever there are human needs to be met."

> "Although compromises may be worked out as a result of a negotiation, the parties should not enter into discussions with the sole intent of compromise."

> "Generally, the parties involved in a negotiation do not *trust* each other. Indeed, the handling of other people's mistrust is the skilled negotiators' stock in trade."

Ashok Kapoor[2] has defined negotiation as the use of common sense under pressure to achieve objectives (which may be more than merely an explicit agreement).

---

[1]Nierenberg, G.I. *Fundamentals of Negotiating.* New York: Hawthorn Books, 1973, p. 5. Used with permission.

[2]Kapoor, A. *Planning for International Business Negotiation.* Cambridge, MA: Ballinger Publishing Company, 1975, pp. 1-3.

According to Kapoor, the nature of international negotiation includes the following dimensions:

Negotiation takes place within the context of the four Cs represented in the second circle in Figure 1.1. The four Cs stand for common interest (something to negotiate for), conflicting interests (something to negotiate about), compromise (give and take on points), and objectives and criteria (determining the objective and the criteria for its achievement).

Figure 1.1 The Context of Negotiation

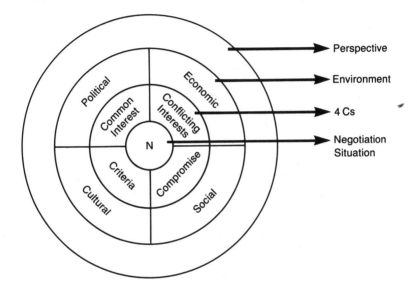

- Negotiation takes place within the context of an environment composed of the political, economic, social, and cultural systems of a country.

- Negotiators must develop a broad perspective that includes the larger context within which they negotiate (e.g., other considerations, similar and related projects, reactions of political and economic interest groups).

- Over time, the four Cs change and the information, know-how, and alternatives available to the negotiating international company and the host country also change, resulting in a fresh interpretation of the four Cs, the environment, and the perspective.

- The unique characteristic of international versus domestic business negotiations is that international negotiations are influenced by a wide diversity of environments. These require changing perspectives that determine the selection of appropriate tactics and strategies of negotiations to be adopted (e.g., concepts of what is right, reasonable, or appropriate, expectations, mood, and reference to one's own cultural values).

Some questions which may be discussed in this context are:

— What was your first intercultural negotiating experience?

— What are the main differences between international and intercultural negotiation?

— Did you experience culture shock? How did you make culture shock work for you?

— Give examples of what is "right," "reasonable," or "appropriate" in North American or European cultures but not so in, say, Asian or Latin American cultures.

INPUT 2

Major Mistakes in Intercultural Negotiations

An effective intercultural negotiator learns from the experiences of others and takes care to avoid major mistakes.

Business negotiations, particularly those involving investment decisions, require deep understanding of the socio-economic and political situation of the host country. There are things which may be sensitive politically. In general, the process of centralized economic planning adopted by many developing countries will require approval of contracts by several function-aries at various diffused centers of power and authority. In many ways, this involves coping with ambiguity and still not losing one's patience. Decision making may be slow without showing any perceptible rational pattern.

There is also the need for building personal relations with key characters in the negotiating process. Trust is generally an important issue. A formal business-like negotiating style may not be enough.

We believe that a good intercultural negotiator, in order to be effective and result-oriented, will avoid the following mistakes:

1. Don't try to look at everything from your own definition of what is "rational" and "scientific."

2. Don't press a point if the other party is not prepared to readily accept it. Wait for a more favourable time.

3. Don't look at things from your own narrow self-interest.

4. Don't ask for concessions or compromises which are politically or culturally sensitive. You will not succeed.

5. Don't stick to your agenda if the other party has a different set of priorities.

6. Don't use jargon which can confuse the other party and create a feeling of distrust.

7. Don't skip authority levels in a way which hurts sensibilities of middle level officials; the top man has the power to commit the organization, but for implementation you require the support of people at intermediate levels.

8. Don't ask for a decision when you know that the other party is not competent to say "yes" or "no".

INPUT 3

The participants can use a tentative comparative study on some basic cultural assumptions that underline the Japanese, North American, and Latin American approaches toward negotiation (Figure 1.2) when they analyze various ways to define negotiation.

Figure 1.2 A Tentative Comparative Study of Cultural Assumptions Related to Negotiation.

ASSUMPTIONS	CULTURES		
	JAPANESE	NORTH AMERICAN	LATIN AMERICAN
1.Emotions	Emotions are valued but must be hidden.	Emotions are not highly valued. Transactions with others are mostly unemotional.	Emotional sensitivity is valued. Interactions can be hightly emotional and even passionate.
2. Power	Subtle power plays. Conciliation is sought.	Power games are played all the time. Litigation, not so much conciliation. To be strong is highly valued.	Great power plays. To be stronger than the others is particularly valued.
3. Decision Making	Group decision making.	Team work provides inputs to decision makers.	Decisions are made by individuals in charge.
4. Social Interaction	Face-saving is crucial. Decisions are often made on the basis of saving someone from embarrassment.	Decisions are made on a cost/benefit basis. Face-saving does not openly matter.	Face-saving for oneself is critical to preserve honor and dignity.
5. Persuasion	Not very argumentative. Quiet when right. Respectful and patient. Modesty and self-restraints are highly valued.	Argumentative when right or wrong. Impersonal when arguing. Practical when presenting arguments.	Passionate and emotional when arguing. Enjoy a warm interaction as well as a lively debate.

6. Readings

1. Casse, P. *Training for the Cross-Cultural Mind.* Washington, D.C. SIETAR, 1981

2. Fisher, G. *International Negotiation: A Cross-Cultural Perspective.* Chicago, Intercultural Press, Inc. 1980.

3. Moran, R.T., and Harris, R.P., *Managing Cultural Synergy.* Houston, Gulf Publishing Company, 1982.

Chapter 2
The Profile of a Successful Intercultural Negotiator

"To strive for perfection is a high ideal. But I say: Fulfil something you are able to fulfil rather than run after what you will never achieve. Nobody is perfect. Remember the saying: None is good but God alone, and nobody can be. It is an illusion. We can modestly strive to fulfil ourselves and to be as complete human beings as possible, and that will give us trouble enough."

C. G. Jung

People differ in their negotiating capabilities. This is natural as our strength as negotiators is a reflection of our total personality and psychic being. If we are able to influence people and their actions under conditions of stress and tension, we can expect to perform well as negotiators. A knowledge of human behavior, generally considered to be an essential attribute, may best be acquired by observing human behavior. Successful negotiators are those who not only monitor behavior of their "opponents," but also exhibit behavioral patterns that facilitate desired outcomes.

In today's complex world, negotiations are generally high in terms of "costs" and "benefits," which explains the effort that goes into achieving mutually acceptable outcomes. While perfection in specific traits is desirable, what is likely to determine the most critical output is the total impact in a given situation. Therefore, to speak of a successful intercultural negotiator is to focus attention on a well-rounded personality, which is sensitive to the needs of intercultural negotiating situations and possesses technical skills and excellence to transform every barrier into a new opportunity for collaborative growth and advancement. And surely such individuals, who are not corporate superstars (people) by any measure, are made, not born, to "win" in difficult negotiations. Today's world needs more of such persons to make it a better place to live and work.

Workshop 2

1. **Aim:** To identify key traits of a successful intercultural negotiator.

2. **Objectives:** Participants will:

(1) Analyze an illustration of psychological differences and its impact on negotiation;

(2) Identify key traits that make a successful negotiator;

(3) Assess their strengths as negotiators and examine some recent research on successful negotiations.

3. Process:

First Exercise. According to Carl G. Jung,[1] there are two psychic attitudes among human beings, namely, extrovert ones and introvert ones. (See brief description below.)

Participants should:

— Analyze the impact of the two psychic attitudes or orientations on the way people negotiate; and

— Examine the negotiation process between extroverted and introverted people.

Extrovert Attitude Type	Introvert Attitude Type
They think, feel, act, and actually live in a way that is directly correlated with the objective conditions and their demands.	They interpose a subjective view between the perception of the object and their own actions, which at times prevents the action from assuming a character that fits the objective situation.
Their life makes it perfectly clear that it is the object and not their subjective view that plays the determining role in their consciousness.	Although they are aware of external conditions, they select the subjective determinants as the decisive ones.
They are open, sociable, jovial, friendly, and approachable.	They are reserved, and very often inscrutable.
They are friendly with everyone or they quarrel with everyone. Get affected by people and their actions.	They are comparatively unaffected by what others say or do.
They expend and propagate.	They defend themselves against certain demands from outside.
Their inner life is subordinated to external necessity.	Their inner life predominates.
They sometimes get sucked into objects and completely lose themselves in them.	Objects have little meaning for them.

[1]Jung, C.G. *Psychological Types*. London: Kegan Paul, 1923.

Second Exercise. The trainer requests the group to come up with a profile of a successful intercultural negotiator. The Group Planning Technique (see conceptual framework: Input 2) is very effective in getting and processing information.

Feedback: In an international workshop (Bombay, 1982), we used the Group Planning Technique and the following profile emerged based on the responses of the group.

Effective negotiators are people who:

1. Understand their objectives clearly

2. Know what the other party wants

3. Are flexible and ready to compromise

4. Understand their own and others' viewpoints

5. Are able to plan and communicate

6. Use a mix of negotiation skills

7. Maintain pressure but keep their cool

8. Are able to present facts effectively

In another Workshop (Manila, 1982), the group came up with a more expanded list incorporating 20 characteristics:

1. Lead the team

2. Communicate effectively (convincing, persuasive, highlight points of mutual interest, etc.)

3. Handle situations tactfully

4. Change strategy whenever necessary

5. Compromise with certain viewpoints of opposite party to arrive at a decision (listen to others' views)

6. Able to assess or evaluate situations

7. Able to make objective decisions

8. Able to maintain good relations

9. Able to size-up the situation and understand alternative courses of action

10. Able to harness their own resources (staff, etc.) for the negotiation

11. Able to understand the needs of other sectors (business, government, etc.)

12. Visualize issues independently and also the relationship between different issues

13. Show flexibility, with a certain range of freedom for discussion

14. Avoid negative reactions in order not to irritate the opposite party

15. Able to offer counter proposals on the spot and reason, question, and summarize

16. Able to put forth their organization's point of view in a clear manner

17. Are diplomatic enough to accept compromise, adjust themselves to different styles, and are sensitive to body language

18. Good strategists and tacticians (soft and hard at the same time)

19. Know the strengths and weaknesses of their team and of the other side

20. Are well prepared for the subject being discussed

Third Exercise. The following self-assessment exercise is intended to give information regarding their intercultural negotiating capabilities to the participants. They must be as spontaneous as possible in answering and must focus on what they believe at the time of the exercise and not what they think their choice should be. They read each "value orientation" and check the appropriate number to the right of the sentence, knowing that the meanings of the numbers used are:

5: I strongly agree

4: I agree

3: I marginally agree

2: I disagree

1: I strongly disagree

Participants must answer all the questions. There are of course no right or wrong answers. The result is for their personal information and guidance and should not be shared with others.

1. I feel that problem solving
can be extremely interesting.   5   4   3   2   1

2. I can manage cultural differences.   5   4   3   2   1

3. I always end my presentation
on a positive and hopeful note.   5   4   3   2   1

4. I respect confidentiality
whenever necessary.   5   4   3   2   1

5.	I am very warm and personal in my communication style.	5	4	3	2	1
6.	I will never underestimate the strength of the other party.	5	4	3	2	1
7.	I take care of unforeseen contingencies.	5	4	3	2	1
8.	I plan my moves well in advance.	5	4	3	2	1
9.	I identify my strong points and use them strategically.	5	4	3	2	1
10.	I am always prepared to compromise (except my objectives).	5	4	3	2	1
11.	I believe in satisfying the needs of all parties.	5	4	3	2	1
12.	I prefer to negotiate with those who have authority.	5	4	3	2	1
13.	I carefully select my seat in a meeting, if possible.	5	4	3	2	1
14.	I know my objectives clearly.	5	4	3	2	1
15.	I believe in strong eye contact.	5	4	3	2	1
16.	I control my body movements and gestures.	5	4	3	2	1
17.	I don't follow disagreements with counter proposals.	5	4	3	2	1
18.	I ask a lot of questions.	5	4	3	2	1
19.	I seek clarification when in doubt.	5	4	3	2	1
20.	I am rigid but willing to move if necessary.	5	4	3	2	1
21.	I am aware of my abilities and limitations.	5	4	3	2	1
22.	I understand the concerns of the other party.	5	4	3	2	1
23.	I am highly persuasive.	5	4	3	2	1
24.	I am patient.	5	4	3	2	1
25.	I know my "costs" and "benefits."	5	4	3	2	1
26.	I like to listen.	5	4	3	2	1

27. I inspire the confidence of people on both sides.	5	4	3	2	1
28. I am prepared to give and take.	5	4	3	2	1
29. I can say "no" effectively.	5	4	3	2	1
30. I like my team members when they perform well.	5	4	3	2	1
31. I like to share new ideas with others.	5	4	3	2	1
32. I like brainstorming sessions.	5	4	3	2	1
33. I can stand tense moments.	5	4	3	2	1
34. I can ease tension with a joke.	5	4	3	2	1
35. I can adjust to sudden shifts in the focus of discussions.	5	4	3	2	1
36. I try hard to reach my goal.	5	4	3	2	1
37. I like taking risks.	5	4	3	2	1
38. I can catch on very quickly.	5	4	3	2	1
39. I can penetrate the real issues.	5	4	3	2	1
40. I make fewer concessions as the deadline approaches.	5	4	3	2	1

Score Sheet

Scores	Negotiating Competence Profile
(a) Less than 40	You could be a loner and live in a world that does not exist outside. *Learn how to learn.*
(b) 40-80	You could possibly do better. Take an inventory of your strengths and weaknesses.
(c) 80-120	You have strong negotiating capabilities. Try to build on them.
(d) 120-160	You are almost an achiever; a little more effort should make you "perfect."
(e) 160-200	You could be a "born" negotiator. There is little chance that you will ever "fail."

4. Time: 4 to 5 hours

5. Conceptual Framework:

INPUT 1

A. Some Psychological Paradigms

Cognitive dissonance is a term coined by Leon Festinger[2] that means an irrational coping behavior caused by two or more contradictory perceptions. For instance, if during the course of negotiation a person pays warm tributes to Japanese innovativeness and high standards of business ethics and at the same time gives the impression that the Japanese are undependable as business partners, that person demonstrates inconsistency between these two beliefs. Successful negotiators normally avoid such contradictions in their belief structures. But there are occasions, more common in intercultural interactions, when dissonance leads to a more balanced perception of reality. This may happen when some new knowledge or perception interferes or conflicts with an old and well established belief. It is painful to reject our pet beliefs; at the same time it is dangerous to ignore new information.

Some very interesting facts have come to light as a result of research in this area:

When choosing among various alternatives, the more attractive the rejected choices, the greater the dissonance arousal. For example; choosing new equipment in the midst of highly competitive bids by Japanese, German, and Italian equipment suppliers. Similarly, the greater the number of rejected alternatives, the greater the dissonance.

If the chosen alternative has some or many negative consequences, dissonance is likely to be greater.

For example, a highly capital intensive investment in a Third World country has a high risk of failure due to limitations of market and other environmental constraints.

Dissonance is aroused when we do something that is in conflict with a belief or an attitude. For example, a Western manager will experience dissonance when working in an alien environment where the "locals" have little or no regard for appointments.

J. A.Hardyck[3] suggests four specific strategies that may be used in reducing dissonance:

— mini-maxing potential gains and losses;

---

[2]Festinger, L.A. *A Theory of Cognitive Dissonance.* Evanston, IL: Row, Peterson, 1957.

[3]Hardyck, J. A. "Predicting Response to a Negative Evaluation." *Journal of Personality and Social Psychology,* 9, Washington D.C.: American Psychology Association, 1968-1969, pp. 128-132.

— preferring to alter weak rather than strong cognitions;

— changing external rather than internal evidence;

— trying to make changes that will be stable over time.

Frustration: This is generally the result of blocking goal attainment or need fulfillment. It is difficult to predict how a particular individual will come to experience frustration. The blockage may be real or imaginary. Sometimes an imaginary blockade leads to frustration, but a real blockade does not. The important determining factor seems to be the manner (rational or irrational) in which the individual treats the situation, i.e. reacts to the developments in the external world.

Regression: This is a retreat into an "earlier" way of dealing with the outside reality and oneself. According to a social psychologist, frustrated people tend to give up constructive attempts at solving their problems and regress to more primitive and childish behavior. In negotiations, regressive behavior may be resorted to by unskilled negotiators who may try to evade unsavoury facts or try to divert their and others' attention from what signifies to them an unpleasant outcome.

Fixation: This may be caused either by frustration or an inflated self-image. It occurs when a person continues to respond to external reality in a manner that has already proved highly ineffective. In other words, the person fails to *switch* and thus fails to cope with the reality. A skilled negotiator is able to switch and thereby explore new ideas and alternatives.

Resignation: This is another name for apathy or a feeling that nothing can be done to save the situation. If the negotiations are protracted, and still do not yield gainful results, negotiators (on both sides) may get the feeling of wasting their time in chasing illusory solutions to the problems.

Repression: Things that we do not like to remember slip into our unconscious mind. These repressed feelings sometime find expression in a number of unrelated ways. We may act too busy to attend a certain meeting, but the real reason may be our dislike for some of the participants. We may suffer a loss or miss an opportunity due to our irrational behavior, but we derive satisfaction from the fact that we heeded "our inner voice."

Projection: This, in simple terms, is attributing one's inner motive to other persons, mostly in an unconscious manner. It is basically a defense mechanism, a "not me" syndrome. "I didn't do this; you did." "I never wished to renegotiate the agreement; you suggested it." And so on. One important point to note is that projection need not be an undesirable reaction all the time. Some people also project their good impulses onto others.

Aggression: Prolonged frustration leads to hostile behavior, not necessarily against the person who had "caused" the frustration in the first place. An aggressive expression in a meeting may take the form of intense body movements and gesticulations. Once the meeting is over, the anger may be directed against persons unconnected with the incident. An experienced negotiator would attempt to defuse the situation instead of escalating it further through matching gestures.

B. Individuation and Negotiation

Below is a brief description of the individuation process as outlined by the Swiss psychologist C. G. Jung.[4]

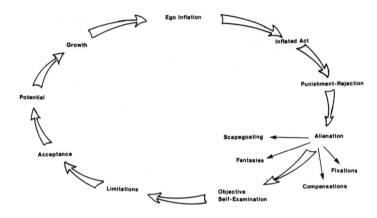

Here are the chronological phases that any negotiator experiences when involved in an attempt to reach an agreement with another party on a matter of mutual interest (note: "he" stands for both male and female negotiators in the following list):

Phase 1. The negotiator believes that he has found "the" solution to the problem under negotiation (ego inflation). He knows he has the answer. Everything is going to be alright. He is ready for a move.

Phase 2. The negotiator makes an offer. Sometimes his proposal is bold. He takes a risk (inflated act).

Phase 3. In many cases the reaction of the other party is not the expected one. As a matter of fact, it's never exactly what was hoped for. The negotiator is taken aback, feels rejected and punished (punishment = rejection).

Phase 4. The negotiator feels bad. He is sorry that he took a risk. The bolder the offer, the more foolish he feels. He has lost control and has the feeling that he has alienated himself. To save face

[4]Jung, C. G. *The Integration of the Personality*. London: Routledge & Kegan Paul, Ltd., 1952.

and survive, he then uses several standard behaviors such as: scapegoating (the other negotiator is crazy, irresponsible), fantasies (nothing happened), compensations (does not say anything anymore, talks too much, starts to overeat, overdrink, oversmoke, flirt), fixations (requests the same offer over and over).

Phase 5.   The negotiator sits back and takes stock. He examines the situation in an objective, neutral way and learns something about himself and others (objective self-examination).

Phase 6.   The negotiator learns something about his own limitations and weaknesses. He has an opportunity to review (and eventually revise) his self-image. He now knows more (and more accurately) about himself (limitations).

Phase 7.   The most painful and difficult step is for the negotiator to accept the fact that he is maybe not the greatest person in the world, that he indeed has shortcomings and weaknesses (acceptance).

Phase 8.   In going through the above process, the negotiator also has an opportunity to learn about his potential, "things" that he owns and was not aware of (potential).

Phase 9.   The negotiator is able to build upon his newly discovered potential. He is in the process of actualizing a new part of himself (growth).

Phase 10.   "And the cycle" (or more exactly "spiral") starts all over again.

INPUT 2

The Group Planning Technique (GPT)

The Group Planning Technique (GPT) is a simple and effective technique to generate new ideas in order to prepare alternative plans of actions and enhance problem solving capabilities. GPT may be used to expand the canvas of options in a situation and to list them in order of their acceptability and feasibility in the decision making process, particularly when problems need immediate and well defined solutions. It is a highly creative activity inasmuch as there is complete participation by all members of the group and the end-result is highly synergistic. Judgments are consciously delayed to explore a complete range of ideas and options.

Prerequisites for successful outcomes: In view of its overall simplicity, GPT does not require high skill levels on the part of the facilitator or the group. Yet there are certain considerations that are important.

(a) Clarity of the problem (avoiding misunderstanding).

(b) The size of the group should not be smaller than 10 or larger than 25.

(c) Members are motivated to "center" attention on the problem.

(d) There is no premature judgment, evaluation, or criticism of ideas.

(e) Silent generation of ideas is encouraged.

(f) Materials required: GPT Idea Generation Worksheet and Idea Selection and Ranking Worksheet as per following specimen format; at least two flip chart stands with sufficient paper markers, masking tape, and pens or pencils for the participants.

(g) Seating arrangement: U-shaped or around a large table. Every participant should be able to watch the facilitator and other participants without any difficulty.

(h) Time required: 1 1/2 hours.

Process: It is important that the following steps in the GPT process are well understood.

(a) Opening statement by the facilitator and reading aloud of the problem. Worksheets are distributed (5 minutes). The wording of the problem (or question) is critical in the process.

(b) Silent generation of ideas by each participant (10 minutes).

(c) Participants meet in small groups (4 to 6) and select what they think the five most important ideas are (30 minutes).

(d) All the small groups share their ideas, which have been written down on flipcharts in a plenary session. No evaluation or criticism is allowed (10 minutes).

(e) Questions are raised by the participants who want some clarification. The facilitator reviews all items and, if the same idea has been repeated, cross-references are indicated in the margin (15 minutes).

(f) Each participant now makes a selection of the five most significant ideas in the master list and ranks them in order of priority using the Idea Selection and Ranking Worksheet. A value of 5 is attached to the idea that is ranked 1 and in descending order the idea ranked 5 has a value of 1.

(g) The facilitator tabulates the results by adding all the individual rankings and a final list of five to ten ideas is prepared (10 minutes).

Ideas Generation Worksheet

Problem: (Example) How would you *negotiate* a promotion for one of your deserving subordinates with your Personnel Director?

1. _____

2. _____

3. _____

4. _____

5. _____

6. _____

7. _____

8. _____

9. _____

10. _____

Ideas Selection and Ranking Worksheet

Idea Number	Rank order	Score for each idea*

* 5 points for the first idea, 4 for the second one, 3 for the third one, 2 for the fourth one, and 1 for the fifth one.

INPUT 3

Chester L. Karrass[5] reports an experiment in which 120 professional negotiators from four major aerospace companies in North America participated. An effort was made to relate the results of negotiation with aspiration

---

[5]Adaptation (pages 15-26) from *The Negotiating Game* by Chester L. Karrass (Thomas Y. Crowell) Copyright© 1970 by Chester L. Karrass. Reprinted by permission of Harper & Row, Publishers, Inc.

level, concession behavior, exploitation of power, skill and success under equal power, skill and success under unequal power, estimating results, settlement time, deadlock, and satisfaction with agreement.

The practical implications of this experiment are summarized below:

1. Higher aspiration level is critical. Negotiators with high aspirations win high rewards. If both the parties have high aspiration levels, the chances of a deadlock are higher.

2. It is better to make large initial demands. Generally, negotiators who make small concessions fail less. Less skilled negotiators tend to make more concessions at the start of the negotiation. It is better to plan concessions in a dynamic way.

3. Power does not guarantee success in negotiations. Power makes a greater difference for unskilled negotiators.

4. Satisfaction with the outcome is not something exclusive to the winners.

The findings of this experiment should be presented and discussed, keeping in mind that they apply mainly to American situations. What about the intercultural dimension? Are they applicable or valid in other cultural environments?

INPUT 4

Since 1968, a number of studies have been carried out by Neil Rackham of the Huthwaite Research Group[6] using behavior analysis methods.

These studies used three success criteria. The successful negotiator:

— is rated as effective by both sides

— has a track record of significant success

— has a low incidence of implementation failure.

A total of 48 negotiators were picked who met all of these success criteria.

The results showed that while there was no significant difference in the overall amount of time spent in planning by skilled and average negotiators, skilled negotiators considered a high number of alternatives per issue; gave more attention to common ground areas than did average negotiators; paid comparatively more attention to long term consideration of anticipated results; set upper and lower limits and planned the objectives in terms of a range as against a fixed point; and placed less reliance on sequence planning (average negotiators begin with point 1, then move to 2, 3, and 4): Skilled negotiators may take up issues in an independent manner.

---

[6]"The Behavior of Successful Negotiators," 1976, Reston, VA: Huthwaite Research Group.

The Huthwaite Research Group also brought out some important factors regarding face-to-face behavior of skilled negotiators. Skilled negotiators avoided words and phrases that caused irritation to the other party. The irritating behavior could include making counter proposals (when they are least expected) and making arguments inadequately backed up by sound reasons. Checking understanding from time to time, asking lots of questions, and sharing feelings in a free manner helped skilled negotiators to achieve their objectives.

6. Readings

1. Fisk, J., and Barron, R. *The Official MBA Handbook.* New York: A. Wallaby Book, 1982.

2. Karrass, C. L. *Give and Take.* New York: Thomas Y. Crowell Co., 1974.

3. Nierenberg, G. I. *Fundamentals of Negotiating.* New York: Hawthorne Books, Inc., 1973.

CHAPTER 3
Pre-Negotiation Planning and Preparation

"If you would work any man, you must either know his nature and fashions, and so lead him; or his ends, and so persuade him; or his weakness and disadvantages, and so awe him; or those that have interest in him, and so govern him. In dealing with cunning persons, we must ever consider their ends, to interpret their speeches; and it is good to say little to them, and that which they least look for. In all negotiations of difficulty, a man may not look to sow and reap at once; but must prepare business, and so ripen it by degrees."

Francis Bacon

Planning is as critical for negotiation as it is for other managerial functions. It helps in many ways, e.g. assessing your tactical strengths and weaknesses vis-à-vis those of the other party; setting objectives in a rational manner and selecting the means of reaching them; providing support systems required; and determining an environment for effective performance. While routine business negotiations may require very little preparatory time, plenty of effort goes into rehearsing a win-win posture for more critical ones. Planning and preparation guidelines would, therefore, include some of the following ingredients:

— Know yourself (self-evaluation)

— Know your opponent (some detective work)

— Set your objectives clearly

— Check your facts and assumptions

— Brainstorm to generate more options

— Plan strategies and tactics

— Rehearse

Planning for negotiation requires both factual and imaginative work. The well prepared negotiator is mostly successful as long as he or she remains flexible enough to adapt to the negotiating situation.

Workshop 3

1. Aim: To stress the importance of planning and preparation in negotiations.

2. Objectives: Participants will:

(1) Identify a set of key considerations in pre-negotiation planning and preparation;

(2) Assess some of the key strengths and weaknesses of a negotiating team; and

(3) Analyze brainstorming and small group consultations as effective techniques for preparing for negotiations.

3. Process:

First Exercise. The following exercise is proposed to two groups of participants: "You are a large, highly technological company in one of the industrialized countries. A parastatal corporation in one of the developing countries wants to put up an industrial project for which your company can supply technical know-how and assist in procurement of equipment. You are aware that another company in your country has the same capabilities and good contacts in the country where the project is to be located. While this would be your first entry into this market, your competitor has executed two projects, one of which had some technical problems during the initial years. Your main strength is the latest advanced technology, while your competitor has some price advantage. A delegation from the parastatal organization is in town with full authority to reach an initial agreement and authorize advance payment for the preparatory work. The chief executive of your company has authorized the high level technology transfer group (of which you are a member) to negotiate the principal terms of the agreement. You have convened a meeting to plan your negotiation. You may use the guidelines below. Your task is to come up with a concrete plan of action with the principal objective of winning this prestigious contract."

The groups are allowed about one hour to complete the planning and preparation. The questions to be discussed during debriefing are:

— How did you go about planning the negotiation? Who was the leader? What leadership style was used? What method was used to generate and test ideas from the group? Who in the group did not support the final outcome and why?

— How optimistic are you, as a group, that you can successfully conclude the negotiation, and what is the basis of this optimism?

— Which substantive factors are common in the presentations of the two groups and which are different?

— In what ways did the guidelines help you in the planning process? What needs to be added or deleted?

GUIDELINES

A set of key considerations in pre-negotiation planning and preparation

---

Stage One: What do we propose to achieve?

Relevant questions to be debated in this regard are:

(1) What is our basic objective?

(2) What is the ideal alternative to achieve that objective?

(3) What are the financial implications?

(4) What are the alternative courses of action (limits of flexibility)?

(5) Who is competing with us?

(6) Do we have enough <u>factual</u> data and information to support our arguments?

Stage Two: How do we go about achieving it?

Relevant questions:

(1) Who will lead the discussion?

(2) Who will check understanding (verify facts)?

(3) What questions should we ask?

(4) What are the emotional issues?

(5) What power do we possess? What power does the other party have?

(6) Who will work to reduce tension and show concern for people

(7) What is the present level of aspiration and what is the required level?

(8) What negotiation styles, strategies, and tactics are we going to use?

Stage Three: What if we fail?

(1) Do we renegotiate?

(2) What "costs" and "benefits" are important?

(3) What new strategies would be available to us?

Second Exercise. The participants identify five resources that a team needs to be effective when negotiating. The exercise is organized in four phases.

Phase 1.   Each participant fills out the following self-assessment exercise (15 minutes).

Assessment Exercise on the
Strengths and Weaknesses of a Negotiating Team

Circle the appropriate score for each item:

When I negotiate I:	Marginally	Somewhat	Very Much
1. Have insights on what to say	1	3	5
2. Document my statements	1	3	5
3. Am sensitive to other people's feelings	1	3	5
4. Plan in advance	1	3	5
5. Remember well what people said during the negotiation	1	3	5
6. Encourage others to express their views	1	3	5
7. Put two and two together very quickly	1	3	5
8. Follow a step-by-step approach	1	3	5
9. Am able to assess the value of the other party's proposals	1	3	5
10. Organize my negotiation in a systematic way	1	3	5
11. Follow my intuition	1	3	5
12. Am perceptive	1	3	5
13. Evaluate my team's expertise	1	3	5
14. Know my "dossier" very well	1	3	5
15. Easily come up with options and alternatives	1	3	5
16. Reason back and forth	1	3	5
17. Am able to determine what is important	1	3	5

18. Look at the negotiation as a win-win situation	1	3	5
19. Am able to put things into perspective	1	3	5
20. Use "logic"	1	3	5
21. Appraise all ideas	1	3	5
22. Can predict the outcome of the negotiation	1	3	5
23. Am aware of the other party's motivation	1	3	5
24. Am able to clarify issues	1	3	5
25. Use various strategies	1	3	5
26. Monitor the progress accomplished	1	3	5
27. Can quote what people said	1	3	5
28. Guess what the other party's next move will be	1	3	5
29. Believe in teamwork	1	3	5
30. Am in favor of using a variety of tactics	1	3	5
31. Offer "deals"	1	3	5
32. Know how to control the negotiation process	1	3	5
33. Enjoy the exchange of ideas	1	3	5
34. Try to understand the other party's position	1	3	5
35. Work all the way through a discussion	1	3	5
36. Bargain	1	3	5
37. Know the facts related to the negotiation	1	3	5
38. Question assumptions	1	3	5
39. Look at the big picture (not the details)	1	3	5

40. Am precise when answering questions	1	3	5
41. Trigger cooperative reactions	1	3	5
42. Propose how to solve problems	1	3	5
43. Project myself into the future	1	3	5
44. Use my experience to back up my arguments	1	3	5
45. Express my emotions	1	3	5
46. See what is right and what is wrong very quickly	1	3	5
47. Am pragmatic	1	3	5
48. Define the negotiating procedures	1	3	5
49. Pinpoint flaws in others' arguments	1	3	5
50. Communicate effectively	1	3	5

Strengths and Weaknesses of a Negotiating Team
Score Sheet

For each item enter the score selected (1 for marginally, 3 for somewhat, and 5 for very much so). The total for each resource cannot be below 10 or above 50. The grand total should be between 50 and 250.

Resource 1.
(Scores)

1	7	11	15	19	22	28	33	39	43	
( ) +	( ) +	( ) +	( ) +	( ) +	( ) +	( ) +	( ) +	( ) +	( ) =	_____

Resource 2.
(Scores)

2	5	14	24	27	35	37	40	44	47	
( ) +	( ) +	( ) +	( ) +	( ) +	( ) +	( ) +	( ) +	( ) +	( ) =	_____

Resource 3.
(Scores)

3	6	12	18	23	29	34	41	45	50	
( ) +	( ) +	( ) +	( ) +	( ) +	( ) +	( ) +	( ) +	( ) +	( ) =	_____

Resource 4.
(Scores)

4	8	10	16	20	25	30	32	42	48	
( ) +	( ) +	( ) +	( ) +	( ) +	( ) +	( ) +	( ) +	( ) +	( ) =	_____

Resource 5.
(Scores)

9	13	17	21	26	31	36	38	46	49	
( ) +	( ) +	( ) +	( ) +	( ) +	( ) +	( ) +	( ) +	( ) +	( ) =	_____

Participants analyze (separately) the results of the self-assessment exercise using the explanation given below:

Resource 1. *Imaginative:* These people are full of ideas: good at using their imagination, following their hunches and inspirations, looking at essentials, identifying options, integrating various pieces of an argument into a meaningful whole, and being inspiring.

Resource 2. *Factual:* These people are always fully prepared for negotiations: good at getting their act together, being precise in their arguments, documenting their statements, knowing their dossiers (including the details), checking the accuracy of the other party's arguments, and explaining the background of the negotiations.

Resource 3. *Relational:* These people are very sensitive about interpersonal relations: good at establishing and maintaining relations, listening, supporting, encouraging, solving conflicts, reducing tension, using confrontations in a constructive way, and being empathetic.

Resource 4. *Analytical:* These people are rational and process-oriented: good at planning a negotiation, establishing the ground rules, setting up an agenda, using various strategies and tactics, being systematic in approaching a problem, arguing in a logical way, and dealing with the "how to" of a negotiation.

Resource 5. *Evaluative:* These people are always weighing the importance, value, and accuracy of the arguments: good at checking, approaching, assuming, controlling, measuring assumptions, monitoring the progress of the negotiation, and identifying what is right and wrong as well as flaws in the arguments of others.

A resource can be underdeveloped (score between 10 and 20), well developed (score between 20 and 40), and overdeveloped (score between 40 and 50).

Phase 2. To be successful, a negotiating team needs a good balance of the five resources. Participants meet in small groups (for 5 minutes) and analyze:

    (1) the profile of their team, assuming that it is a negotiating one;

    (2) the strengths and weaknesses of their team; and

    (3) the action needed to prepare themselves for the negotiation (how are they going to build on their strengths and reduce their weaknesses?) that is going to take place between their team and another team (see the instructions below).

Instructions for half of the teams

"Prepare all the arguments you can think of to justify the death penalty."

Instructions for the other half of the teams

"Prepare all the arguments you can think of to justify the abolition of the death penalty."

Phase 3. Teams meet two by two and negotiate for 30 minutes. At the end of the negotiation a vote in favor or against the death penalty is taken. The trainer then asks the teams to:

    (1) see if they were able to convince some members of the other negotiating team to change their minds and join them;

    (2) review their effectiveness as a negotiating team.

Phase 4. The following questions are discussed with the participants:

— What happens when a team has too many imaginative, factual, rational, analytical, evaluative members?

— When in the negotiation should a team use the various resources it has?

— Could you illustrate the various resources with some practical examples?

Third Exercise. Participants read the following instructions:

Assume that you are about to participate in an important negotiation concerning your future growth in the organization you work for. Since the outcome is critical, you decide to approach the problem in a systematic way in order to handle the situation in an effective manner.

The process goes like this. You work on your own for about 15 minutes applying the systematic framework to the negotiation situation. After this you will meet with a few other participants for consultation. You will present your analysis and perceptions to get their reactions. The other participants who have also worked on their negotiating situations will make similar presentations and get feedback from the small groups in which you will participate as a consultant. (Please see Conceptual Framework Input 3 for a note on Small Group Consultations.) The process will be completed when all the participants have shared their planned approaches to negotiation. This may take from 30 minutes to 1 hour depending on the total number of participants in each group. The four steps in systematic approach are given below.

STEP 1:   SITUATION ANALYSIS

— What is the situation?

— Is it clear or ambiguous?

— What are the supporting and opposing forces?

STEP 2:   KNOW YOURSELF

— Where do you stand as of now?

— Where would you like to be?

— What are your strengths and weaknesses?

STEP 3:   CLARIFY OBJECTIVES

— Why do you negotiate?

— What is the outcome you are working to achieve?

— Write down a clear statement of your objective.

— What alternatives are available to you to achieve the objective?

STEP 4:   KNOW THE OTHER PARTY

— Who is the other party?

— What is your past experience?

— What are the major distinctions in terms of needs and priorities?

— Is there a common ground?

— What are your major weak points which you must cover against?

4. Time: About 4 hours.

5. Conceptual Framework:

INPUT 1

Participants answer the following questions individually and then discuss their answers in small groups.

Think   (1) of a negotiation you were involved in and that went very well;

(2) of a negotiation that failed.

Identify as many cues as possible to document your two assessments. Use the following tasksheet to answer the questions (Figure 3.1).

**Figure 3.1 Criteria for Assessing Negotiation
(Task Worksheet)**

INDICATORS OF SUCCESSFUL NEGOTIATION	INDICATORS OF UNSUCCESSFUL NEGOTIATION

INPUT 2

Brainstorming

Brainstorming is a spontaneous and nonevaluative technique of generating innovative and creative ideas. It is effective in problem solving and generation of alternatives. The process is highly productive and synergistic. It saves time and ensures involvement of a group of people to resolve a complex situation. The main objective of a brainstorming session is to generate new options. This becomes possible as all criticism and evaluation is postponed until the end. The success of the session, however, depends on the skill of the facilitator, a clear statement of session objectives, availability of a flip chart, an informal friendly atmosphere, and a small but highly creative group of people.

After the brainstorming is over, evaluation of ideas may be undertaken in stages. We must look at the positive and negative side of each idea. What can go wrong if we accept it? Who foots the bill for this additional cost? What strategic advantage do we gain by following this path? And so on. The options may be narrowed down to a small, easily manageable number. Another concern that a skilled negotiator would have at the end of this exercise is how to relate these options within the overall tactical and strategic framework. Options devoid of this framework would not place you in a win-win situation.

INPUT 3

Small Group Consultation

Small Group Consultation (SGC) is a process whereby a few individuals (4 to 6), who share an identity of interest, attempt to gain a deeper insight into their life positions or problems through open sharing of feelings and perceptions in an informal and largely unstructured setting.

The process may be divided into FOUR distinct phases:

Phase 1.   Building a relationship of trust and confidence. Members accept the fact that mutual sharing is indeed helpful and healthy.

Phase 2.   Presenting the experience or problem in an authentic manner; i.e., disclosure of all the necessary information that is important for other members of the group to react in a positive way.

Phase 3.   Listening and responding. Carefully listening and absorbing the feedback. Seeking and offering clarification whenever necessary. This is also the learning phase.

Phase 4.   Building upon others' ideas and preparing for the exit with new or reinforced solutions to the problems discussed with the group members.

6. Readings

1. Kapoor, A. *International Business Negotiations.* New York: New York University Press, 1970.

2. Karrass, C.L. *The Negotiating Game.* New York: Thomas Y. Crowell Co., 1970.

3. Nierenberg, G.I. *The Art of Negotiating.* New York: Cornerstone Library, 1968.

CHAPTER 4
Negotiation Skills
and Types

"The harder you push yourself, the harder yourself is likely to push back. And that can make you damn tired."

S. Herman

According to our experience in the negotiating field, four factors have to be kept in mind when one tries to improve one's own negotiation effectiveness:

1. People who do not share the same cultural assumptions and values find it very difficult to understand each other and practice empathy. Most people in most cultures have not been culturally "programmed" to identify what separates them. Many negotiations fail because the parties involved are not able to recognize their different ways of looking at the same thing and avoid value judgments.

2. Many negotiators are unable to confront their differences at the time they arise. Usually they wait until the ambiguity and resentment are such that any agreement or settlement is impossible.

3. The practical reasons for negotiation breakdowns are related to a lack of clarification regarding the roles of the parties involved, some weakness in the communication between the parties involved, the inability to deal with conflicts, and the inability to manage the negotiating process.

4. Unfocused negotiation creates embarrassment and frustration that lead to individuals' self-centered behavior such as withdrawing, fighting, giving up, or becoming dependent.

No one is born a perfect negotiator. We can learn to change, to acquire the skills needed to negotiate effectively, and to improve in applying the skills in day-to-day social interactions.

Workshop 4

1. Aim: To experience some practical ways to improve one's own negotiating effectiveness.

2. Objectives: Participants will:

(1) Analyze five intercultural negotiating skills;

(2) Define three different types of negotiations;

(3) Apply the negotiating skills and types to various intercultural situations.

3. Process:

First Exercise. An exercise on intercultural skill is proposed to the group.[1]

Instructions: Assume that you have to select someone who is going to represent your group in an international (intercultural) negotiation and proceed as follows:

Step 1. Meet in pairs and rank (1 being the most important and 5 the least important) the five proposed intercultural negotiation skills (see Figure 4.1). You have 15 minutes to accomplish your task.

Step 2. Now meet with another pair and negotiate a common ranking of the same five skills. You have 30 minutes to reach complete agreement. You will be recorded[2] during the entire negotiation.

Step 3. Meet for debriefing.

Figure 4.1 The Five Intercultural Negotiating Skills

Rank the following:

• *Skill A:*	to be able to practice empathy and to see the world as other people see it. To understand others' behavior from their perspective.
• *Skill B:*	to be able to demonstrate the advantages of what one's proposals offer so that the counterparts in the negotiation will be willing to change.
• *Skill C:*	to be able to manage stress and cope with ambiguous situations as well as unpredictable demands.
• *Skill D:*	to be able to express one's own ideas in such a way that the people one negotiates with will objectively and fully understand what one has in mind.
• *Skill E:*	to be sensitive to the cultural background of the others and adjust the suggestions one wants to make to the existing constraints and limitations.

---

[1]Casse, P. *Training for the Cross-Cultural Mind.* Washington, D.C.: SIETAR, 1981, p. 154.

[2]Each negotiation is taped or videotaped.

During debriefing, various rankings are identified and discussed. The score sheet below (Figure 4.2) is also used to: (1) see who has "won" or who has "lost", and (2) analyze *why* some teams changed their ranking.[3]

Figure 4.2 Intercultural Negotiations Skills Exercise Score Sheet

	Your Original Ranking	Negotiated Ranking	Team Change
A.	_____	_____	_____
B.	_____	_____	_____
C.	_____	_____	_____
D.	_____	_____	_____
E.	_____	_____	_____

Total
Change
Score
(absolute difference between ranking
and negotiated ranking)

Following the above exercise, a presentation on "three types of negotiation" (with their advantages and disadvantages) is made:

Figure 4.3 Three Types of Negotiation

TYPES	ADVANTAGES	DISADVANTAGES
1. Negotiations based on *Compromise.* (Someone gives up something.)	Enables the negotiators to overcome deadlocks, to move forward and faster.	Risk of frustration for the one who gave up something. Lack of commitment on his (her) part to the final decision.
2. Negotiations based on *Synthesis.* (All the ideas are taken into account.)	The negotiators try to integrate all the individual's ideas in the final agreement. This type leads to motivation and commitment.	Sometimes irrelevant elements are included in the decision and that can make the outcome of the negotiation weaker, more questionable.
3. Negotiations based on *Synergy.* (Creativity is the key to effective negotiation.)	The outcome of the negotiation is the real product of the interaction between the negotiators who are creative. It is typical of a win-win situation.	This type of negotiation requires time, flexibility, and open minds.

[3]Process designed by Dr. D. Berlew.

When the three types of negotiation have been introduced to the group, the trainer asks the participants to identify the type(s) used by them during the negotiation of the five intercultural negotiating skills.

Participants are also asked to comment (with illustrations) on the following pattern of negotiation:

Phase 1.   Synthesis: Many negotiators first try to integrate all the ideas into one joint proposal agreeable to all.

Phase 2.   Synergy: Confronted with the difficulty of coming up with one fully integrated proposal, the negotiators start to explore new avenues.

Phase 3.   Compromise: Because of the time pressure (as well as other constraints), the parties involved are now turning to a "give-and-take" process.

Second Exercise. Since *listening* is critical in any negotiation, a self-assessment exercise on negotiation and listening skills is provided to the participants.[4]

---

[4]Adapted from Moran, R. T., and Harris, R. P. *Managing Cultural Synergy*. Houston, Tx: Gulf Publishing Company, 1982, pp. 88-89. Used with permission.

Figure 4.4 A Self-Assessment Exercise on Listening Skills

RATE YOUR LISTENING ABILITIES

	Almost Always	Usually	Occasionally	Seldom	Almost Never
1. Do you put what you've been doing out of sight and out of mind when negotiating?	5	4	3	2	1
2. Do you look at the other party?	5	4	3	2	1
3. Do you ignore the distractions around you?	5	4	3	2	1
4. Do you smile, nod your head, and otherwise encourage the "opponent" to talk?	5	4	3	2	1
5. Do you think about what the negotiator is saying?	5	4	3	2	1
6. Do you try to figure out what the negotiator means?	5	4	3	2	1
7. Do you try to figure out why the negotiator is saying it?	5	4	3	2	1
8. Do you let the negotiator finish what he or she is trying to say?	5	4	3	2	1
9. If the "opponent" hesitates do you encourage him or her to go on?	5	4	3	2	1
10. Do you re-state what the negotiator has said and ask if you got it right?	5	4	3	2	1

(continued)

(continued)

	5	4	3	2	1
11. Do you withhold judgment about the other party's idea until he or she is finished?	5	4	3	2	1
12. Do you listen regardless of the other party's way of speaking and choice of words?	5	4	3	2	1
13. Do you listen even though you anticipate what the other party is going to say?	5	4	3	2	1
14. Do you question the negotiator in order to get him or her to explain ideas more fully?	5	4	3	2	1
15. Do you ask the other party what his or her words mean, imply?	5	4	3	2	1

Participants add their scores to arrive at a total. They can be interpreted according to three categories of scores:

1. For scores between 60 and 75: the assessee is indeed very good at listening to others (too good maybe?).

2. For scores between 30 and 60: some improvements can be made.

3. For scores between 15 and 30: the assessee definitely has a listening problem.

Third Exercise. A series of short negotiation exercises are proposed to the group:

(A) Participants meet in threes and look for a solution to a given problem (see below) using a three step approach:

(1) Identify the negotiation skills and types you are going to utilize to solve the problem;

(2) Apply the skills to the problem at hand; and

(3) Prepare a brief report for the entire group.

Instructions To The Participants

As an international team of experts working in a developing country, you have been amazed to see the old people, bent over with short brooms, sweeping their houses.

Sweeping in that position several hours a day is somewhat painful and ineffective.

You have decided to help the people and to introduce the use of a broom with a long handle.

The problem is how to convince them to change their habits.

(B) A critical incident is given to the group for discussion.

Instruction For The Participants

Assuming that you are Mr. Kemper, how would you approach the following negotiation and why?[5]

At 8.04 a.m., the intercom bleeped.

"Mr. Kemper" said the secretary in a lowered voice, "there are four cabin cleaners in reception — blacks — and they insist on seeing you. They seem to be angry."

---

[5]*The Art of Japanese Management* copyright 1981 by Richard Tanner Pascale and Anthony G. Athos, reprinted by permission of Simon & Schuster, Inc.

Mr. Kemper paused, drumming his fingers on the stacks of papers that had brought him to work an hour early, before his day of nonstop meetings began. "Sounds like one we'd better deal with," he replied. "Send them in." For Larry T. Kemper, regional manager of United Airlines, overseer of 20,000 employees in the western United States and eight organizational levels removed from the hourly cabin cleaners he was about to encounter, the day had begun.

Cabin cleaners are among the lowest paid and least skilled airline employees. Their occupation involves hours of waiting, punctuated by frenzied bursts of activity when, working on tight turnabout schedules, they pour through the planes, cleaning out seat pockets, ashtrays, galleys, and restrooms. The grievance that the contingent wished to communicate was that their white foreman consistently assigned them the most unpleasant jobs. They wanted him to change that.

(C) Participants meet in small groups of five or six and answer the question:

"The skills that a negotiator should use in order to be effective depend on . . ."

(D) Participants are split into groups of three and their members must select a performer, a responder, and an observer. When ready, the performers leave the room while the responders get their instructions. A rotation system is used so that everybody has a chance to experience the three roles:

— *The performer* has to discuss a topic for 3 or 4 minutes without knowing what the responder is trying to achieve;

— *The responder* has to practice some negotiating skills (one at a time and for each round) in a subtle way so that the performer is influenced without being aware of what is going on;

— *The observer* watches the performer's reactions or the impact of the responder's behavior on the performer. The observer leads the discussion on what happened during the exercise when the round is over.

For each round, a conventional or unconventional negotiating skill is presented to the responder. (He or she will have to practice that skill during the exercise.) The performer comes back and has three minutes to discuss in a free way a given topic (see Figure 4.5) with the responder. After the discussion with the observers, the trainer briefly lectures on the pros and cons of the skill just experienced (see Conceptual Framework: Input 3).

**Figure 4.5 The Practice of Conventional and Unconventional
Negotiating Skills**

SKILLS	TOPICS FOR DISCUSSION *The performer should talk about:*
1. CONVENTIONAL — Paraphrasing (reformulate what the other party said using your own words).	— Three ways to prepare a negotiation.
— Using silence (do not say anything after a question or right after a statement made by the other party. Wait a while).	— Five ways to prepare a negotiation effectively.
— Using open-ended questions (ask questions that start with what, who, when, why and that cannot be answered by a yes or no).	— The best way to assess a negotiator's effectiveness.
2. UNCONVENTIONAL — Misunderstanding (in a systematic but subtle way, do not understand what the other party talks about).	— How to start a negotiation so that there is a fair chance that it will succeed.
— Exaggerating (amplify everything the other party says. Use expressions such as always, sooner, everybody, no one, impossible).	— Five ways to monitor the progress accomplished during a negotiation.
— Avoiding (do not talk about the given topic. Make sure that the performer talks about something else).	— Negotiation is manipulation.

4. Time: Half a day to one full day.

5. Conceptual Framework:

INPUT 1

Figure 4.6   A Basic Model on Negotiation and Ambiguity

All negotiations are ambiguous at times

Ambiguity can lead to:

(1)   (2)

Tension and *Frustration* in many cultures of the Western world	*Flexibility* and *Creativity* in many cultures of the Eastern world

The typical reaction following the experience of ambiguity, tension, and frustration are:

— Withdrawing

— Adapting

— Being aggressive

The typical reactions following the experience of flexibility and creativity are:

— Becoming committed

— Exploring new avenues

— Accommodating

INPUT 2

Figure 4.7 Three Approaches Toward Negotiation and Their Related Skills

Human Relations Approach	Gestalt Approach	Provocative Approach
Principle:	**Principle:**	**Principle:**
To *understand* each other is critical for the success of the negotiation	To be *authentic* about one self is what determines the quality of a negotiation	To *provoke* to get reactions and adjust accordingly is the motto of this approach
Skills:	**Skills:**	**Skills:**
Ability to practice *empathy* (conventional skills)*	Ability to handle *conflicts* in a straightforward way (unconventional skills)*	Ability to push, surprise, and manipulate (unconventional skills)*

*See Conceptual Framework: Input 3: Figure 4.8

INPUT 3

Figure 4.8 Advantages and Disadvantages of the Conventional and Unconventional Negotiating Skills

SKILLS	PROS	CONS
1. Paraphrasing	Helps to clarify one's own understanding of what the other person said, check accuracy of the received message, and show interest in others.	Can upset the other party if he or she gets the impression that the negotiation is a one-way street process.
2. Using silence	"Forces" the other party to answer question or *add* something to a comment that he or she has already made.	Can be embarrassing or completely ineffective in certain cultures.
3. Using open-ended questions	Enables the negotiator to get more information on a subject of interest to him or her.	Some questions can be perceived as offending, especially the ones starting with "why."

(continued)

4. Misunderstanding	Leads the other party to clarify his or her ideas, to provide some extra information to reinforce his or her arguments.	Can upset some people who cannot see why they are not understood. It can trigger some tension and frustration.
5. Exaggerating	Preempts any kind of action the negotiator knows the other party is ready to take. It also forces the person one negotiates with to fine tune his or her arguments.	The other party gets emotional and eventually angry at the negotiator.
6. Avoiding	Triggers some creativity and synergy since the other party has to integrate his or her arguments into a different, new framework.	This can be so depressing for the other party that in some cases he or she will simply withdraw from the negotiation.

INPUT 4

Negotiation Skills[6]

Successful negotiation . . ., requires a set of skills which must be learned and practiced. These skills include (1) the ability to determine the nature of the conflict, (2) effectiveness in initiating confrontations, (3) the ability to hear the other's point of view, and (4) the utilization of problem-solving processes to bring about a consensus decision.

Diagnosis

Diagnosing the nature of a conflict is the starting point in any attempt at resolution through negotiation. The most important issue which must be decided is whether the conflict is an ideological (value) conflict or a "real" (tangible) conflict — or a combination of both. Value conflicts are exceedingly difficult to negotiate. If, for example, I believe that women should be treated as equals in every phase of public and private life, and you believe they should be protected or prohibited in certain areas, it would be very difficult for us to come to a position that would satisfy us both.

A difference of values, however, is really significant only when our opposing views affect us in some real or tangible way. If your stand on women's place in society results in my being denied a job that I want and am qualified

---

[6]Reprinted from: J. William Pfeiffer and John E. Jones, Editors. *The 1974 Annual Handbook for Group Facilitators,* San Diego, CA. Copyright 1980, University Associates, Inc. Used with permission.

to perform, then we have a negotiable conflict. Neither of us needs to change his values for us to come to a mutually acceptable resolution of the "real" problem. For example, I may get the job but, in return, agree to accept a lower salary or a different title or not to insist on using the all-male executive dining room. If each of us stands on his principles — maintaining our value conflict — we probably will make little headway. But if, instead, we concentrate on the tangible effects in the conflict, we may be able to devise a realistic solution.

The Israeli-Arab conflict provides a good example of this point. In order to settle the tangible element in the conflict — who gets how much land — ideological differences do not need to be resolved. It is land usage that is the area of the conflict amenable to a negotiated settlement.

It is important to determine whether a conflict is real or a value conflict. If it is a conflict in values resulting in nontangible effects on either party, then it is best tolerated. If, however, a tangible effect exists, that element of the conflict should be resolved.

Initiation

A second skill necessary to conflict resolution is effectiveness in initiating a confrontation. It is important not to begin by attacking or demeaning the opposite party. A defensive reaction in one or both parties usually blocks a quick resolution of differences. The most effective way to confront the other party is for the individual to state the tangible effects the conflict has on him or her. For example: "I have a problem. Due to your stand on hiring women as executives, I am unable to apply for the supervisory position that I feel I am qualified to handle." This approach is more effective than saying, "You male chauvinisit pig — you're discriminating against me!" In other words, confrontation is not synonymous with verbal attack.

Listening

After the confrontation has been initiated, the confronter must be capable of hearing the other's point of view. If the initial statement made by the other person is not what the confronter was hoping to hear, defensive rebuttals, a "hard-line" approach, or explanations often follow. Argument-provoking replies should be avoided. The confronter should not attempt to defend himself, explain his position, or make demands or threats. Instead, he must be able to engage in the skill termed reflective or active listening. He should listen and reflect and paraphrase or clarify the other person's stand. When the confronter has interpreted his opposition's position to the satisfaction of the other person, he should again present his own point of view, being careful to avoid value statements and to concentrate on tangible outcomes. Usually, when the confronter listens to the other person, that person lowers his defenses and is, in turn, more ready to hear another point of view. Of course, if both persons are skilled in active listening, the chances of successful negotiation are much enhanced.

Problem-Solving

The final skill necessary for successful negotiation is the use of the problem-solving process to negotiate a consensus decision. The steps in this process are simply stated and easy to apply. (1) Clarifying the problem. What is the tangible issue? Where does each party stand on the issue? (2) Generating and evaluating a number of possible solutions. Often these two aspects should be done separately. First, all possible solutions should be raised in a brainstorming session. Then each proposed solution should be evaluated. (3) Deciding together (not voting) on the best solution. The one solution most acceptable to all parties should be chosen. (4) Planning the implementation of the solution. How will the solution be carried out? When? (5) Finally, planning for an evaluation of the solution after a specified period of time. This last step is essential. The first solution chosen is not always the best or most workable. If the first solution has flaws, the problem-solving process should be begun again at Step 1.

Since negotiation is the most effective of all conflict-resolution strategies, the skills necessary to achieve meaningful negotiation are extremely important in facing inevitable conflicts.

6. Readings

1. Athos, A.G., and Pascale, R.T. *The Art of Japanese Management.* New York: Warner Books, 1981.

2. Bellenger, L. *L'Argumentation.* Paris: Les Editions E.S.F., 1980.

3. Huthwaite Research Group. "The Behaviour of Successful Negotiators", Situation Management Systems, Inc., 1976.

CHAPTER 5
Negotiation Styles

"The world with which literature deals is the world into which human beings are born and live and finally die; the world in which they love and hate; in which they experience triumph and humiliation, hope and despair; the world of sufferings and enjoyments, of madness and common sense, of stillness, cunning and wisdom, the world of social pressures and individual impulses, of reason against passion, of instincts and conventions, of shared language and unshareable feeling and sensation; of innate differences and the rules, the roles, the solemn or absurd rituals imposed by the prevailing culture. Every human being is aware of this multifarious world and knows (rather confusedly in most cases) where he stands in relation to it. Moreover, and, by analogy and himself, he can guess where other people stand, what they feel and how they are likely to behave."

Aldous Huxley

Style is a manner of speech and writing that is characteristic of the person who is using it. It lends grace and polish to the person's actions or manners. We make choices when we speak or write but surprisingly these choices can also be a matter of habit. We acquire a particular style due to habitual ways of responding to the external reality; our thoughts and feelings also shape our entire personality.

Our negotiating style reflects the way we cope with the changes in our environment. No style is good or bad, effective or ineffective. It depends on the situation in which we are placed. By and large, our negotiating effectiveness is a function of our ability to switch from one style to another. A critical factor in negotiation is to know what styles we feel more comfortable with and to learn how to identify other people's styles. The more able we are to use various styles, the more efficient we become.

Workshop 5

1. **Aim:** To help particpants to understand their own and others' negotiating styles with a view to improving their negotiating effectiveness.

2. **Objectives:** Participants will:

(1) Identify four negotiating styles as well as four modes of negotiation;

(2) Learn how to cope with different styles and learn how to switch from one style to another;

(3) Experience the negotiation process between two cultures.

3. Process:

First Exercise. This exercise is made up of eight phases:

Phase 1.   A self-assessment exercise is completed by the participants. No explanation is given about the meaning of IN, NR, AN, and FA at this time.

Negotiation Styles
A Self-Assessment Exercise[1]

Please respond to this list of statements in terms of what you believe you do when negotiating with others. Base your answers on your typical day-to-day activities. Be as frank as you can.

For each statement, please enter on the score sheet that follows the number corresponding to your choice of the five possible responses given below:

1. If you have NEVER (or very rarely) observed yourself doing what is described in the statement.

2. If you have observed yourself doing what is described in the statement OCCASIONALLY, BUT INFREQUENTLY: that is, less often than most other people who are involved in similar situations.

3. If you have observed yourself doing what is described in the statement about AN AVERAGE AMOUNT: that is, about as often as most other people who are involved in similar situations.

4. If you have observed yourself doing what is described in the statement FAIRLY FREQUENTLY: that is, somewhat more often than most other people who are involved in similar situations.

5. If you have observed yourself doing what is described in the statement VERY FREQUENTLY: that is, considerably more than most other people who are involved in similar situations.

Please respond to each statement using numbers 1-5 (see above). Use score sheet on page 58.

1. I focus on the entire situation or problem.

2. I evaluate the facts according to a set of personal values.

3. I am relatively unemotional.

4. I think that the facts speak for themselves in most situations.

[1]An adaptation of the Interactive Style Questionnaire developed by Situation Management Systems, Inc., Huthwaite Research Group.

5. I enjoy working on new problems.

6 I focus on what is going on between people when interacting.

7. I tend to analyze things very carefully.

8. I am neutral when arguing.

9. I work in bursts of energy with slack periods in between.

10. I am sensitive to other people's needs and feelings.

11. I hurt people's feelings without knowing it.

12. I am good at keeping track of what has been said in a discussion.

13. I put two and two together quickly.

14. I look for common ground and compromise.

15. I use logic to solve problems.

16. I know most of the details when discussing an issue.

17. I follow my inspiration of the moment.

18. I take strong stands on matters of principle.

19. I am good at using a step-by-step approach.

20. I clarify information for others.

21. I get my facts a bit wrong.

22. I try to please people.

23. I am very systematic when making a point.

24. I relate the facts to experience.

25. I am good at pinpointing essentials.

26. I enjoy harmony.

27. I weigh the pros and cons.

28. I am patient.

29. I project myself into the future.

30. I let my decisions be influenced by my personal likes and wishes.

31. I look for cause and effect.

32. I focus on what needs attention now.

33. When others become uncertain or discouraged, my enthusiasm carries them along.

34. I am sensitive to praise.

35. I make logical statements.

36. I rely on well tested ways to solve problems.

37. I keep switching from one idea to another.

38. I offer bargains.

39. I have my ideas very well thought out.

40. I am precise in my arguments.

41. I bring others to see the exciting possibilities in a situation.

42. I appeal to emotions and feelings to reach a "fair" deal.

43. I present well articulated arguments for the proposals I favor.

44. I do not trust inspiration.

45. I speak in a way which conveys a sense of excitement to others.

46. I communicate what I am willing to give in return for what I get.

47. I put forward proposals or suggestions which make sense even if they are unpopular.

48. I am pragmatic.

49. I am imaginative and creative in analyzing a situation.

50. I put together very well-reasoned arguments.

51. I actively solicit others' opinions and suggestions.

52. I document my statements.

53. My enthusiasm is contagious.

54. I build upon others' ideas.

55. My proposals command the attention of others.

56. I like to use the inductive method (from facts to theories).

57. I can be emotional at times.

58. I use veiled or open threats to get others to comply.

59. When I disagree with someone, I skillfully point out the flaws in the other's argument.

60. I am low-key in my reactions.

61. In trying to persuade others, I appeal to their need for sensations and novelty.

62. I make other people feel that they have something of value to contribute.

63. I put forth ideas which are incisive.

64. I face difficulties with realism.

65. I point out the positive potential in discouraging or difficult situations.

66. I show tolerance and understanding of others' feelings.

67. I use arguments relevant to the problem at hand.

68. I am preceived as a down-to-earth person.

69. I go beyond the facts.

70. I give people credit for their ideas and contributions.

71. I like to organize and plan.

72. I am skillful at bringing up pertinent facts.

73. I have a charismatic tone.

74. When disputes arise, I search for the areas of agreement.

75. I am consistent in my reactions.

76. I quickly notice what needs attention.

77. I withdraw when the excitement is over.

78. I appeal for harmony and cooperation.

79. I am cool when negotiating.

80. I work all the way through to reach a conclusion.

Negotiation Styles
Score Sheet

Enter the score you assign each question (1, 2, 3, 4, or 5) in the space provided. *Please note:* the item numbers progress across the page from left to right. When you have all your scores, add them up vertically to attain four totals. Insert a "3" in any number space left blank.

1. _____	2. _____	3. _____	4. _____
5. _____	6. _____	7. _____	8. _____
9. _____	10. _____	11. _____	12. _____
13. _____	14. _____	15. _____	16. _____
17. _____	18. _____	19. _____	20. _____
21. _____	22. _____	23. _____	24. _____
25. _____	26. _____	27. _____	28. _____
29. _____	30. _____	31. _____	32. _____
33. _____	34. _____	35. _____	36. _____
37. _____	38. _____	39. _____	40. _____
41. _____	42. _____	43. _____	44. _____
45. _____	46. _____	47. _____	48. _____
49. _____	50. _____	51. _____	52. _____
53. _____	54. _____	54. _____	56. _____
57. _____	58. _____	59. _____	60. _____
61. _____	62. _____	63. _____	64. _____
65. _____	66. _____	67. _____	68. _____
69. _____	70. _____	71. _____	72. _____
73. _____	74. _____	75. _____	76. _____
77. _____	78. _____	79. _____	80. _____
IN: _____	NR: _____	AN: _____	FA: _____

Phase 2. The following negotiation exercise is now given to the participants who use a cassette recorder to tape their negotiation.

The Negotiating Meeting Exercise

The situation

You are planning your participation in a *negotiating meeting*. Although you do not know anything about what is going to be negotiated, you have been asked to organize the meeting so that it will be as effective as possible.

The Task

You will find on the next page twenty activities (A through T) related to the organization of a negotiating meeting and presented at random. Your task consists in rank ordering the activities so that they are placed in a logical order. Start with 1 for the first activity, then 2 for the second one, and so on until 20 for the logical last sequence.

The process

Step 1: Take 30 minutes to rank order the twenty activities by yourself.

Step 2: Meet in teams of four and take 60 minutes to reach a consensus on one common, joint ranking (do not vote and do not change your individual rankings as determined under step 1). Do not forget to *tape* the entire session.

Step 3: The trainer provides the ranking of "experts" in the negotiating field (see figure 5.1). Write that ranking under step 3.

Step 4: Determine your individual scores by subtracting the experts ranking from your ranking (in absolute terms without taking the minuses and pluses into consideration) and adding up the differences.

Step 5: Your team (four people) should now determine its score by subtracting the experts' ranking from your own team ranking. Add up the differences (in absolute terms) to find the total team score.

Step 6: Calculate the average of your individual scores by dividing the total of your individual scores by the number of team members (four).

Step 7: Assess your gain or loss scores in comparing the team scores with the average of the individual scores. If the team score is lower than the average individual score, then the gain score is positive. It the team score is higher than the average individual score, then the gain score is negative.

Step 8: Identify the lowest score for your team.

Step 9: See how many individual scores are lower than the team score.

Step 10: Determine if your negotiation was *SYNERGISTIC* or not:

(a) the higher the gain score the more synergistic the negotiation;

(b) the more individuals' scores are lower than the team score, the less synergistic the negotiation is.

NEGOTIATING MEETING ACTIVITIES	Step 1 Individual Ranking	Step 2 Team Ranking	Step 3 Experts' Ranking	Step 4 Difference Between Steps 2 and 3	Step 5 Difference Between Steps 1 and 3
A. Agree with the participants in the meeting on the time available					
B. Introduce each other					
C. Conclude the meeting					
D. Invite the participants to the meeting					
E. Open the meeting					
F. Present and get the agenda of the meeting approved					
G. Decide on improvements for further meetings					
H. Prepare for the meeting (why a meeting?)					
I. Welcome the participants					
J. Compare the meeting results against the planned objectives					
K. Check the meeting room					
L. Send the minutes of the meeting to the participants					

(continued)

NEGOTIATING MEETING ACTIVITIES	Step 1 Individual Ranking	Step 2 Team Ranking	Step 3 Expert's Ranking	Step 4 Difference Between Steps 2 and 3	Step 5 Difference Between Steps 1 and 3
M. Introduce the purpose of the meeting					
N. Go through the agenda point by point					
O. Clarify the objectives of the meeting with the participants					
P. Prepare the documents to be used in the meeting					
Q. Check the accuracy of the minutes of the meeting					
R. Decide on the working methods (how to) with the participants					
S. Set up an action plan to be implemented after the meeting					
T. Distribute the responsibilities among the participants at the meeting					

Figure 5.1 Expert's Ranking

1. Prepare for the meeting (why a meeting?)   (H)

2. Invite the participants to the meeting   (D)

3. Check the meeting room   (K)

4. Prepare the documents to be used in the meeting   (P)

. . . .

5. Open the meeting   (I)

6. Welcome the participants   (E)

7. Introduce each other   (B)

8. Introduce the purpose of the meeting   (M)

9. Clarify the objectives of the meeting with the participants   (O)

. . . .

10. Present and get the agenda of the meeting approved   (F)

11. Agree with the participants in the meeting on the time available   (A)

12. Decide on the working methods (how to) with the participants   (R)

13. Distribute the responsibilities among the participants at the meeting   (T)

. . . .

14. Go through the agenda point by point   (N)

15. Set up an action plan to be implemented after the meeting   (S)

16. Conclude the meeting   (C)

. . . .

17. Check the accuracy of the minutes of the meeting   (Q)

18. Compare the meeting results against the planned objectives.   (J)

19. Send the minutes of the meeting to the participants   (L)

20. Decide on improvements for further meetings   (G)

Phase 3. The theory regarding the four negotiating styles and four modes of negotiation is provided to the group and the participants are asked to relate it to their negotiation style profile (Figure 5.2). The trainer can use (1) the tally sheets for negotiating styles (Figure 5.3) and modes (Figure 5.4), and (2) the Conceptual Framework: Input 1, to present the theory on negotiation styles and modes.

Figure 5.2 Negotiation Style Profile

Now enter your four scores from the negotiating styles self-assessment exercise on the bar chart below. Construct your profile by connecting the four data points.

	UNDERUSED	PROPERLY USED	OVERUSED
INTUITIVE STYLES			
NORMATIVE STYLE			
ANALYTICAL STYLE			
FACTUAL STYLE			

20 25 30 35 40 45 50 55 60 65 70 75 80 85 90 95 100

Figure 5.3 Tally Sheet For Negotiating Styles

Four Styles	Negotiating Partners*			
1. Factual: *Basic Assumption:* "The facts speak for themselves." *Behavior:* Pointing out facts in a neutral way, keeping track of what has been said, reminding people of their statements, knowing most of the details of the discussed issue and sharing them with others, clarifying, relating the facts to experience, being low-key in their reactions, looking for proof, documenting their statements. *Key Words:* meaning, define, explain, clarify, facts.				
2. Intuitive: *Basic Assumption:* "Imagination can solve any problem." *Behavior:* Making warm and enthusiastic statements, focusing on the entire situation or problem, pin-pointing essentials, making projections into the future, being imaginative and creative in analyzing the situation, switching from one subject to another, going beyond the facts, coming up with new ideas all the time, pushing and withdrawing from time to time, putting two and two together quickly, getting their facts a bit wrong sometimes. Being deductive. *Key Words:* principles, essential, tomorrow, creative, idea.				

(continued)

*Identify the four negotiating partners and put a check in the appropriate place each time that you hear something that is typical of a style.

3. Normative: *Basic Assumption:* "Negotiating is bargaining." *Behavior:* Judging, assessing and evaluating the facts according to a set of personal values, approving and disapproving, agreeing and disagreeing, using loaded words, offering bargains, proposing rewards, incentives, appealing to feelings and emotions to reach a "fair" deal, demanding requiring, threatening, involving power, using status, authority, correlating, looking for compromise, making effective statements, focusing on people, their reactions, judging, attentive to communication and group processes. *Key Words:* wrong, right, good, bad, like.					
4. Analytical: *Basic Assumption:* "Logic leads to the right conclusions." *Behavior:* Forming reasons, drawing conclusions and applying them to the case in negotiation, arguing in favor or against one's own or others' position, directing, breaking down, dividing, analyzing each situation for cause and effect, identifying relationships of the parts, putting things into logical order, organizing, weighing the pros and cons thoroughly, making identical statements, using linear reasoning, being inductive. *Key Words:* because, then, consequently, therefore, in order to.					

Figure 5.4 Tally Sheet for Negotiating Modes

Four Modes	Negotiating Partners*				
1. *Moving against or pushing* Take the initiative, explain, lead, confirm, define, argue, appeal, attack, challenge, being *pro-active.*					
2. *Moving with or pulling* Listen, ask questions, build upon others' ideas, solicit information, reflect back others' feelings, being *re-active.*					
3. *Moving away or avoiding* Avoid contact, confrontation, conflict; change the subject, use silence, talk about something else, *by-passing.*					
4. *Not moving or letting be* Observe, watch, focus on the here and now, act as an observer, is not involved, think about something else, do not respond to questions, being *passive.*					

*Identify the four negotiating partners and put a check in the appropriate place each time you hear something on the tape that is typical of a mode.

Phase 4. The recorded cassettes are played back, the participants learn how to identify various negotiation styles using the tally sheets for negotiating styles and modes.

Phase 5. The group is split into small groups and the participants have to find out the "right" answers (according to each style) using the following statements:

STATEMENTS	TYPICAL ANSWERS ACCORDING TO FOUR STYLES
1. Your boss says: "Sorry, but you have to rewrite your report."	1. *Factual style.* You say: "What do you mean by rewriting? Which parts do I rewrite? Do you have guidelines that I can use?"
2. The representative of the government says: "Frankly, I would like to go ahead with the project we are talking about, but I believe that my country is already too much involved in too many projects."	2. *Intuitive sytle.* You say: "Don't you see that this project fits into your overall program . . . look at the advantages . . It is a good investment!"

3. Your secretary says: "I am terribly upset about the fact that I am the only one in this unit who works overtime. Sorry, but I cannot type your tables. They will have to wait."	3. *Analytical style:* You say: "Let's see who is doing what right now. Well, if you do not type them we are going to be late and that will lead to . . ."
4. One of the team members says: "I do not want to work with Mr. X."	4. *Normative style:* You say: "What's wrong with X? I think you're making a mistake. Do it for the last time."

Phase 6.   Four teams are given the following assignment:

Brainstorm and identify the respective advantages and disadvantages of each style:

Team 1 works on the *factual style,* which is quite often effective when the situation requires a clarification of the available information. (What is it?)

Team 2 works on the *intuitive style,* which is particularly indicated when a set of objectives (projections into the future) have to be identified. (What could it be?)

Team 3 works on the *analytical style,* which can be used to explore different strategies to achieve the agreed upon objectives. (How do we get there?)

Team 4 works on the *normative style,* which is helpful when a decision (evaluation) has to be made. (How important is it?)

The teams repeat the same exercise for the other negotiating *modes.*

Phase 7.   The same teams are requested to set up guidelines about how to cope with other negotiating styles. They compare their suggestions with the guidelines produced by other groups (Figure 5.5).

Figure 5.5   Guidelines For Negotiating With People Having Different Styles

1. *Negotiating With Someone Having a Factual Style*

    *Be *precise* in presenting your facts.

    *Refer to the *past* (what has already been tried out, what has worked, what has been shown from past experience, etc.).

    *Be *inductive* (go from the facts to the principles).

    *Know your dossier (including the details).

    *Document what you say.

2. *Negotiating With Someone Having an Intuitive Style*

    *Focus on the situation as a whole.

*Project yourself in the future (look for opportunities).

*Tap the imagination and creativity of your partner.

*Be quick in reacting (jump from one idea to another).

*Build upon the reaction of the other person.

3. *Negotiating With Someone Having an Analytical Style*

*Use logic when arguing.

*Look for causes and effects.

*Analyze the relationships between the various elements of the situation or problem at stake.

*Be patient.

*Analyze various options with their respective pros and cons.

4. *Negotiating With Someone Having a Normative Style*

*Establish a sound relationship right at the outset of the negotiation.

*Show your interest in what the other person is saying.

*Identify his or her values and adjust to them accordingly.

*Be ready to compromise.

*Appeal to your partner's feelings.

Phase 8.   *Track Exercises.* The purpose of this part of the Workshop is to learn how to switch from one style to another.

Step 1.   Participants meet in threes.

Step 2.   Each participant identifies his or her *primary style* (i.e., the style with which he or she feels most comfortable). The trainer announces that three exercises are going to be given and that each member of the group will have an opportunity to practice (in an exaggerated or Gestalt way) his or her primary style with another member while the thrid member will play the role of an observer.

It should be clarified that:

a. The primary style should be identified and presented to the other team members before knowing what the exercise is going to be.

b. Each round of the exercise will last 5 minutes.

c. The "performer" should overdo it in terms of using his or her primary style.

    d. The member who responds to the "performer" does not have to use a particular style.

    e. After each round, the observer will provide some feedback on what happened. Four minutes will be devoted to a discussion on the outcome of the interaction.

The trainer is now ready to present the exercises one by one:

First Round: A friend and colleague of yours told you that your boss is not happy about your performance. You decide to go and see your boss to discuss the issue.

Second Round: You have been invited by the boss of your boss to meet with him and discuss your request for a promotion. Present your case to him.

Third Round: You have just learned that a colleague of yours is taking full advantage of a project you successfully initiated. You decide to have a conversation with that colleague.

Step 3. The participants select the styles wtih which they feel the least comfortable (or underdeveloped styles) and practice the same way they did with their primary styles.

First Round: You must inform one of your subordinates that his or her performance is very weak.

Second Round: Express your view briefly on a controversial topic about which you feel strongly. Try to convince your counterpart of the validity of your position.

Third Round: You feel very strongly that your talents are unrewarded. You meet with your boss to discuss the matter.

Step 4. This time the performer does not reveal which style(s) he or she is going to use during the exercise. It is up to the second member of the group to (a) identify the style(s) used; and (b) try to adjust accordingly.

First Round The performer tells you that he/she cannot repay the loan borrowed from your bank due to uncertain business conditions.

Second Round The performer is a civil servant in a developing country. He/she will persuade the Finance Minister to liberalize import policy.

Third Round. Try to convince your counterpart that you are getting a lot out of this Workshop.

Second Exercise. Slow Motion Exercise:[2]

Participants are requested to rank (individually) the five negotiating tactics that follow according to their importance in relation to cross-cultural negotiation.

Five Negotiation Tactics:

- Find common ground as quickly as possible
- Explore the differences
- Get a "yes" as quickly as possible
- Overwhelm the other party with facts and data
- Be flexible

Participants *plan* their negotiation and the slow motion exercise begins when they are ready to negotiate with another member of the group who has a different ranking. The rules of the simulation are:

1. Each pair has 30 minutes to reach a consensus and a common understanding.

2. No verbal interaction is allowed. The tally sheet provided (Figure 5.6) has to be used back and forth between the two negotiators (see below).

3. The messages are decoded by the two negotiators according to the four negotiating styles and four modes when the exercise is over.

4. Participants share their findings.

---

[2]Originally created by Dr. D. Berlew.

Figure 5.6 Tally Sheet For Slow Motion Exercise

SENDER	RECEIVER	MESSAGE	DECODING*

*To be used to identify the various styles and modes used during the negotiation when the exercise is over.

Third Exercise **The Red-Blue Culture Exercise.**[3] The purpose of the exercise is to give the group an opportunity to experience the negotiation process between two different microcultures (the Red and Blue cultures). More specifically, participants will check the impact of some basic assumptions regarding the objectives of the negotiation, trust, conflict, power, and decision making on negotiating.

Process

1. The facilitator splits the group into two negotiating teams that meet in two different rooms. Two observers for each team are also selected.

2. He or she explains that the exercise is about negotiation between two cultures. The tally sheet is given to each team *without* any explanation. The tally sheet (Figure 5.7) is reproduced on a flipchart so that everybody can focus on the same information. The two teams have 10 minutes to clarify the given information. The facilitator is ready to answer any questions they may have. The checklist for observers is also distributed (Figure 5.8). It is pointed out that observers cannot interfere during the exercise. They are free to move around.

3. The facilitator clarifies the fact that Rounds 4, 7, and 10 are preceded by a 5-minute negotiation. It means that each team will have to select a representative (not necessarily the same one for each round), and send him or her to the negotiation meeting which will take place in a third room.

4. It is important to leave complete freedom to the two teams as far as the clarification of the purpose of the exercise is concerned. However, questions regarding who selects what and the meaning of the various possible combinations should be thoroughly answered.

5. Round 1 begins and after three minutes the decisions made by the two teams are written on flipcharts. Then the groups move to round 2 and so on.

6. Rounds 4, 7, and 10 consist of a 5-minute negotiation between two representatives of the Red and Blue cultures and a 3-minute decision making session.

7. Round 10 is followed by the announcement of the final decision.

8. Since this exercise can be "heavy" at times and lead to sensitive reactions, the debriefing part is *critical*. At least *one hour* should be devoted to the processing of what has happened. Observers should report first. Participants should feel free to say whatever they want and clarify all issues they have identified.

---

[3]Reprinted from: J. William Pfeiffer and John E. Jones, Editors. *A Handbook of Structured Experiences for Human Relations Training, Volume III,* San Diego, CA. Copyright 1974, University Associates, Inc. Used with permission.

The facilitator will identify the key points from time to time and relate them to *real life situations.*

Some of the issues that may be discussed during the debriefing are: (see also Conceptual Framework: Input 4)

— Clarification of objectives

— Trust or mistrust

— Conflict

— Power

— Decision making

— The meaning of winning and losing

— Taking risks

— Using a mediator (third party)

— Competition

— Leadership

— Preconceptions (influence of past experience on the negotiating process)

— Breaking negotiation

— Short-term versus long-term gains

Figure 5.7 Tally Sheet for Negotiation Between Two Cultures

Blue Culture

	X	Y
A	+3 / +3	+6 / −6
B	−6 / +6	−3 / −3

Red Culture

AX: Both teams win 3 points
AY: Red loses 6 points, Blue wins 6 points
BX: Red wins 6 points, Blue loses 6 points
BY: Both teams lose 3 points

ROUND	MINUTES	CHOICE		CUMULATIVE POINTS	
		RED	BLUE	RED	BLUE
1	3				
2	3				
3	3				
4*	5 = Negotiation 3 = Decision				
5	3				
6	3				
7**	5 = Negotiation 3 = Decision				
8	3				
9	3				
10**	5 = Negotiation 3 = Decision				

*Payoffs are doubled for this round (Negative remains negative)
**Payoffs are squared for this round (Negative remains negative)

Figure 5.8 Negotiation Exercise. Checklist for Observers

Questions	Content	Process
(1) Did the group clarify its objectives?	What did they *want* to achieve through negotiation?	How did they clarify their objective? (once and for all, or . . .)
(2) What was the impact of trust (or mistrust) on the negotiation process?	Did the trust issue come up during the negotiation?	How did the group handle this issue?
(3) What about some basic assumptions regarding:		
— Conflict	Was there any conflict?	How was it handled by the group?
— Power	Was there any power confrontation (power game) during the negotiation?	How was the power used during the negotiation?
— Decision making	What were the key decisions?	Who made the decisions? How?

4. Time: Between 10 and 12 hours.

5. Conceptual Framework

INPUT I

Psychological Types (C.G. Jung)
and Negotiating Styles

According to C.G. Jung, there are two different ways of preceiving or getting information from the inner or outer world into our psyche.

The Psychic Compass: Two Perceiving Functions

SENSES

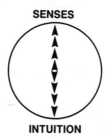

INTUITION

(a) *Senses.* We can use our five senses to identify reality (we hear, see, smell, touch, and taste). When we approach a situation using our sensing function, we try to be factual, objective, neutral, and as accurate as possible. We focus upon the facts. We try to understand what is as it is. We are present-oriented.

(b) *Intuition.* We can also use our imagination to observe what's going on. In this case, we use our imagination and go beyond the facts to guess the ultimate realities. We look for possibilities and opportunities that are inherent to the situation. We project ourselves into the future.

According to the same model, the mind also has two different approaches regarding the treatment or processing of information: the *thinking* and *feeling* functions.

(a) *Thinking.* We process the information collected through our senses and intuition in a logical, neutral, objective, analytical, systematic, and "scientific" way. One compares, differentiates, abstracts, specifies, etc.

(b) *Feeling.* We process data using our values to assess their relevance and importance: we like or don't like, it is good or bad, right or wrong, important or not. The collected information is weighed according to one's own value system. It colors our evaluation of emotions and sensitivity. It makes us human.

The Psychic Compass: Two Processing Functions

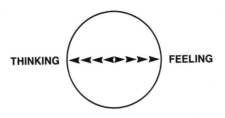

The Complete Psychic Compass⁴

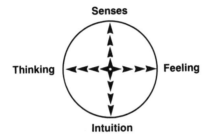

The four dominant psychic functions detemine the nature of *negotiation styles:*

PSYCHIC FUNCTIONS	NEGOTIATING STYLES
Sensing	Factual
Intuition	Intuitive
Thinking	Analytical
Feeling	Normative

1. *FA or Factual Style.* People using the factual style are cool, collected, patient, down-to-earth, present-oriented, precise, realistic, able to document their statements, sticking to the facts that speak for themselves.

2. *IN or Intuitive Style.* This style is characterized by a charismatic tone, a holistic approach (the entire situation is reviewed at the same time),

---

⁴For more information on the psychic compass as defined by C.G. Jung, consult: I. Progoff. *Jung's Psychology and its Social Meaning.* New York: Anchor Books, 1973, pp. 86-99.

a strong imagination, a tendency to jump from one subject to another, a lot of ups and downs, a fast pace, a deductive way to approach problems as well as a future orientation.

3. *NR or Normative Style.* For those who use this style negotiating is basically bargaining. They judge, assess, and evaluate the facts according to a set of personal values. They appeal to feelings, offer bargains, propose rewards and incentives. They look for compromises.

4. *AN or Analytical Style.* The basic assumption that underlies this style is that "logic leads to the right conclusions." These people form reasons, analyze each situation in terms of cause and effect, put things into a logical order, weigh the pros and cons, use a sort of linear reasoning. They are unemotional and focus upon the relationship of parts.

Four Modes of Negotiating

Any individual can use his or her psychic energy in four different ways when negotiating:

1. Moving against or *pushing.*

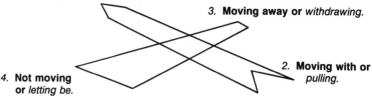

3. Moving away or *withdrawing.*

2. Moving with or *pulling.*

4. Not moving or *letting be.*

(1) *Moving against or pushing:* Explain, demonstrate, take the lead, repeat, clarify, confirm, define, express feelings, argue, appeal, judge, disagree, attack, pinpoint flaws, challenge, keep pressing.

(2) *Moving with or pulling:* Listen, build upon others' ideas, agree, summarize, paraphrase, solicit criticism, look for common ground, appreciate, be relaxed, pay compliments, ask open-ended questions, show understanding, ask for opinions and suggestions, admit lack of understanding.

(3) *Moving away or withdrawing:* Avoid confrontation, contact, conflict; change the subject, use silence, do not answer questions, passive reactions, be fatalistic.

(4) *Not moving or letting be:* Observe, watch, focus on the here and now, flow with the forces around, wait and see.

INPUT 2

This input is geared at helping the participants in the workshop to learn how to identify some of the weaknesses (related to the use of styles) of the people they have to negotiate with.

The approach to be used can be described as follows:

1. Identify the dominant negotiating style of the other negotiator;

Figure 5.9 Shadow Styles And Negotiation

SHADOW STYLES	SHORTCOMINGS
1. **FACTUAL** (opposite to intuitive)	— Impatient with details — Not precise in presenting data — Unrealistic and not very practical — Rely on inaccurate information — Not good at answering pointed questions Others*
2. **INTUITIVE** (opposite to factual)	— No imagination — Procrastinate because he or she cannot reach any conclusions — Cannot see the big picture. Get lost in details — Rely on previous experience too much — Have problems with meanings of words and symbols Others*
3. **ANALYTICAL** (opposite to normative)	— Accept new ideas without checking — Lack validity from a logical viewpoint — Mix up ideas, things and people — Use illogic ways to reason — Overcriticize others' analysis — Become subjective and partial Others*
4. **NORMATIVE** (opposite to analytical)	— Enjoy tough arguments and confrontation — Lack tactfulness — Have problems in relating to others — Make mistakes in assessing the values of things and ideas — Over emotional Others*

*Others to be added by the participants

2. Concentrate on the opposite style to the dominant one. This is the underdeveloped or *SHADOW* negotiation style; one the other negotiator feels uncomfortable with;

3. Meet in threes and determine (a) why you should use the other negotiator's shadow style? (b) when in the negotiation? and (c) how? (Use the four descriptions provided in Figure 5.9.)

INPUT 3

Participants who share the same dominant negotiating style meet and clarify its impact on planning, decision making, conflict-resolution, teamwork, etc.

Figure 5.10 provides a framework for gathering information on the impact of negotiating styles on managerial activities, such as planning, decision making, conflict resolution, and teamwork.

Figure 5.10 Negotiating Styles and Their Cultural Features

	FACTUAL	INTUITIVE	ANALYTICAL	NORMATIVE
1. **Planning**	Focus on the *present,* here and now; on what is in the current problems and issues; on what has to be done *right now.*	Focus on the *future;* on what next; on short-, medium- and long-term issues; on what has to be done today to prepare for the future.	Relate *past, present,* and *future.* Select priorities and identify pros and cons for each of them.	Focus on the *past;* on the assessment of past actions, or who should do what and the impact of the decided actions on people.
2. **Decision Making**				
3. **Conflict Resolution**				
4. **Teamwork**				

6. Readings

1. Glenn, E.S., Withmeyer D., and Stevenson, K.A. "Cultural Styles of Persuasion." *International Journal of Intercultural Realations.* Fall 1977, Vol. 1., No. 3, p. 52.

2. Jung, C.G. *Psychological Types.* Princeton, NJ: Bollington Series, Princeton University Press, 1976.

3. Lawrence, G. *People, Types and Tiger Stripes.* Gainsville, FL: Center for Applications of Psychological Types, Inc, 1982.

CHAPTER 6
Negotiation Strategies and Tactics

"In all fighting, the direct method may be used for joining battle but indirect methods will be needed to secure victory."

Sun Tzu

Strategy: A well thought out game plan; a calculated and planned effort to achieve a given set of goals or objectives.

Tactics: A set of highly skillful acts performed with a degree of finesse for gaining an advantage in terms of positions envisaged in a plan.

Maneuvers: Unanticipated and sudden movements or shifts or diversions of short duration aimed at securing tactical gains in a combative situation.

Technique: A tested method or mode or approach based on theoretical and/or pragmatic considerations, employed for the purpose of attaining a level of performance that one is able to forecast in a rational manner.

If the negotiating table is the place where people find negotiated solutions to problems, its sanctity is best preserved by carefully planning each important negotiation comprising possible solutions to problems and evaluating their favorable or undesirable consequences. The planning process enables us to generate and weigh diverse options. It also helps us in deciding upon the best possible strategy that ensures attainment of the most desired outcome. The lack of strategy or strategic planning would make us move back and forth only to serve ends that are of doubtful utility.

Our ability to excel in making tactical moves, maneuvering, or sophisticated techniques is a valuable asset, but for more enduring gains these should not only appear but also work like parts of a strategic whole. A skilled negotiator is always a skilled strategist. The game plan is perfected in terms of objectives to be met, options available, areas of agreement or conflict, and the most beneficial or rewarding outcome(s). This "perfection," however, does not preclude sudden and unanticipated changes in objectives, or discovery of new options and more beneficial outcomes than what was envisaged at the planning stage. This perspective is important inasmuch as flexibility during negotiations strengthens our negotiating postures without radically departing from what we set out to achieve in the first place.

Workshop 6

1. Aim: To understand the role and importance of strategy and tactics in the negotiating process.

2. Objectives: Participants will:

(1) Examine the Harvard Method of Principled Negotiation as a strategic approach to planning and conducting negotiations;

(2) Apply a set of tactics and maneuvers during simulated negotiations;

(3) Learn effective use of negotiation techniques, particularly use of questions, and of listening and responding skills.

3. Process:

First Exercise

Step 1. The facilitator will make a brief presentation explaining the Harvard Method of Principled Negotiation (Conceptual Framework: Input 1).

Some of the questions that could be discussed are:

- Do you think that the Harvard Model would work in cultures outside North America? Does it work in North America?

- How do you separate the people from the problems as mostly people themselves are a problem?

- Why not follow a soft or hard or principled approach depending on the situation? What are the limitations of a situational approach?

- What other methods could be used besides brainstorming to "invent options"?

- Fisher and Ury have tried to answer three questions:

  (1) What if they are more powerful?

  (2) What if they won't play?

  (3) What if they use dirty tricks?

- Are there any other approaches drawn from your own cultures to effectively handle such situations?

- What other strategic approaches have you effectively employed during negotiations?

Step 2. The group members have an opportunity to practice the three strategies outlined by Fisher and Ury (Harvard Model):

Phase 1. The group is split into three teams (teams 1, 2, and 3);

Phase 2. Each team is assigned a strategy (soft, hard, or principled);

Phase 3. The following negotiating situation is provided to the three teams:

> "The Chief Executive of a multi-cultural organization (5,000 people) has decided to replace the obsolete and ineffective performance appraisal system based on 'Management by Objectives' by a much more straightforward approach. He has asked you (experts in personnel management) to outline a negotiating strategy to be used with the very powerful organizational union."

Phase 4. In 45 minutes, each team has to prepare the requested outline assuming that:

Team 1 will use the soft approach;

Team 2 will use the hard approach;

Team 3 will use the principled approach.

Phase 5. Each team presents its report in a plenary session (30 minutes).

Second Exercise. Participants look at the typology developed by Marwell and Schmitt[1] and discuss in groups of four what the best strategy(ies) would be for the situations briefly described on the following pages:

---

[1]Burgoon, M., Dillard, J. P., Doran, N. E., and Miller, M. D. "Cultural and Situational Influences on the Process of Persuasive Strategy Selection." *International Journal of Intercultural Relations.* Vol. 6, Number 1, 1982.

Figure 6.1 Marwell and Schmitt Typology of Compliance Gaining Strategies

Strategy	Example
Promise	If you comply, I will reward you.
Threat	If you do not comply, I will punish you.
Expertise (positive)	If you comply, you will be rewarded by the "nature of things."
Expertise (negative)	If you do not comply, you will be punished by the "nature of things."
Liking	Actor is friendly and helpful to get target in good frame of mind so that he will comply.
Pregiving	Actor rewards target before requesting compliance.
Aversive stimulation	Actor continuously punishes target making cessation contingent on compliance.
Debt	You owe me compliance because of past favors.
Moral appeal	You are immoral if you do not comply.
Self-feeling (positive)	You will feel better about yourself if you comply.
Self-feeling (negative)	You will feel worse about yourself if you do not comply.
Altercasting (positive)	A person with "good" qualities would comply.
Altercasting (negative)	Only a person with "bad" qualities would not comply.
Altruism	I need your compliance badly so do it for me.
Esteem (positive)	People you value will think better of you if you comply.
Esteem (negative)	People you value will think worse of you if you do not comply.

Situation 1

You have to negotiate with people from a culture in which the following ideas are highly valued:

(a) To *win* is the only negotiating objective;

(b) You cannot *trust* people. If you do, they take advantage of you;

(c) *Compromises* are perceived as weaknesses by most people.

Situation 2

The people you have to negotiate with believe that:

(a) The most important thing in negotiation is to make sure that nobody *loses face*;

(b) Negotiation takes time. It is an *ongoing process*;

(c) Negotiation by *consensus* is the most effective way to reach agreements on matters of mutual interest.

Situation 3

You meet with a team of negotiatiors who:

(a) Are *emotional*;

(b) Do not know their *facts*;

(c) Are *status oriented*.

Third Exercise. Participants experience a simulation on negotiating tactics and maneuvers.

(1) The facilitator divides the group into three teams.

(2) Each team receives one set of negotiating tactics and maneuvers: Set 1 (CE), Set 2(CH), and Set 3 (DU). They read them before the negotiating situation is described to them. The meanings of CE, CH, and DU are not explained at this stage.

(3) Teams spend the first 15 minutes understanding the practical implications of the tactics/maneuvers assigned to them.

(4) After the discussion is concluded, the facilitator announces the negotiating situation (below). Each team is allocated one of the three roles.

(5) Teams prepare themselves for the negotiation using the tactics and maneuvers outlined in their respective instructions (30 minutes).

(6) A tripartite negotiation is held (15-20 minutes).

(7) The facilitator processes the simulation explaining use of tactics and maneuvers by various teams. The facilitator also clarifies the meaning of CE *(clean and effective),* CH (requiring *careful handling),* and DU *(dangerous and unethical).*

(8) Some of the issues that may be discussed during debriefing are:

- Using tactics and maneuvers to further predetermined strategic goals;

- Psychological impact of "dirty" tactics and maneuvers;

- Tactical switching;

- Negotiating style, mode, strategy, tactics, and maneuvers of the "winning team."

The Negotiating Situation

The government of a developing country is concerned about the slow and tardy implementation of rural development projects. The three parties involved are: (a) government officials; (b) local professionals; and (c) overseas experts representing international agencies and foreign governments. The negotiation will center around:

- Inter-agency coordination

- Cost reduction and controls

- Project scheduling

- Involvement of villagers in development projects

- Supplies and administrative support.

It is important to understand the perceptions of these parties and their attitudes towards each other:

Government officials and local professionals think that overseas experts:

- are unable to tune in to local conditions and tend to look upon all problems from a Western viewpoint;

- are entitled to liberal salaries and perks far in excess of what local officials receive and consequently have a different lifestyle;

- tend to spend more time at the project headquarters in the capital than at the project site;

- face communication problems due to their inability to speak and understand the local language;

- consider themselves accountable only to donor countries/lending agencies;

- show little regard to local cultural sensibilities;

- lack the desired depth of commitment.

Government officials have some reservations regarding local professionals too. They seem to:

- be urban oriented;

- show little regard for rules and procedures;

- be more concerned with carrying on with the job rather than being committed to the socioeconomic significance of the projects;

- be too demanding in terms of facilities and support systems;

Both local professionals and foreign experts find government officials to be:

- too domineering, bureaucratic, arrogant, procedure oriented, slow moving, and at times totally indifferent to the problems faced in the field;
- slow in according necessary approvals and releasing funding in local currency;
- ineffective in providing and coordinating support of the local agencies/ authorities.

Negotiation Tactics and Maneuvers Inventory

Set 1 — CE

1. Know what you want, but stay flexible

2. Know your opponent

3. Look for common ground

4. Maintain pressure; avoid provocation

5. Identify multiple currencies of exchange (listen attentively, identify others' needs and wants, explain, prove, express true feelings, summarize, and build trust)

6. Match needs and priorities

7. Check negative consequences of settlement

8. Counsel — leave the room to counsel with associates whenever it will be useful

9. Use silence — silence is the best reply to a totally unacceptable offer

10. Humor — inject humor or suggest a break

11. Positive outlook — do not end a meeting on a negative note

12. Reason responses — do not react too unfavorably to your own mistakes

13. Leave — when the mission is accomplished, leave

14. Forebearance — patience pays

15. Participate — enlist the aid of other parties on your behalf to act either directly or indirectly

16. Status quo — static and changeless condition

17. Open inspection — full freedom to examine

18. Fair and reasonable

Set 2 — CH

1. Surprise — a sudden shift in method, argument, or approach

2. *Fait accompli* — "possession is nine-tenths of the law"

3. Apparent withdrawal — attack and retreat

4. Bland withdrawal — walk out

5. Reversal — going forward and backward

6. Limits or deadline — communication limits, time limits, geographical limits, etc.

7. Foreign — apparent move in one direction to divert attention from the real goal or object

8. Association or halo effect

9. Disassociation — avoiding unsavory association

10. Blanket — shotgun coverage or try to cover as large an area as possible to achieve a breakthrough in one or more places

11. Randomize — make use of the law of chance to defeat the *bluffing advantage* in a game

12. Random sample — pick a sample and assume that the sample that has been chosen will represent the whole

13. Salami or nibbling — a slice at a time

14. Bracket — do not spend all of the decision time trying to be *right on target;* be satisfied to be in the right area and therefore cutting down the degree of error

15. Agency — allow an agent to conduct your negotiations for you

16. Shift levels — change involvement in the problem to a higher or lower level

17. Stretch out — delay until uncertainty is reduced

18. Limited inspection — controlled access

19. Confession — full disclosure

20. Qualified confession — limited answers to questions

21. No admittance — complete security of records

22. United Nations — broad-based alliance of interested parties

23. Arbitration — third party decision, impartial or biased

24. Budget bogey — package to price consideration

25. Intersection — simultaneous negotiations of multiple and divergent contracts

26. Chinese auction — negotiate with more than one party so that each knows that the others are being considered favorably

27. Big brother — benevolence based on high status

28. Little brother — charity desired on the basis of lower status

29. Long lost brothers — search for relationship and status

30. Brinkmanship — the art or practice of pushing a dangerous situation to the limit of safety before stopping

31. Denial — retraction of statement

Set 3 — DU

1. Phony facts — false statistics and errors

2. Ambiguous authority

3. Personal attacks

4. Good guy/bad guy routine — sugar and spice role play

5. Refuse to negotiate

6. Escalate demands

7. Hardhearted partner — "I am willing but my partner is not"

8. Take it or leave it

9. Bribery — payoffs and collusion

10 Approval — mandatory approval designed to impede agreement

11. Escalate approval — deliberate imposition of sequential higher approval veto

12. Missing man — deliberate absence of person with final authority

13. Blackmail — pay or else

14. Scrambled eggs — create deliberate add-ons and changes

15. Scoundrel — deliberate larceny by never-ending renegotiation

3. Time: 8 to 10 hours.

4. Conceptual framework:

INPUT 1

The Principled Method of Negotiation

This model rejects two traditional approaches to negotiation, soft and hard. The soft approach is effective inasmuch as it produces results quickly, but it usually leads to unwise agreements and victimization of the performers. In many situations, being nice is no answer. The hard approach is basically a win-lose situation. It invariably leads to positional bargaining, is time consuming, endangers personal relationships, and is worse if there are many parties.

Roger Fisher and William Ury of the Harvard Negotiating Project[2] present an alternative in the form of principled negotiation, which is based on two assumptions:

- Participants are problem solvers;

- The goal is a wise outcome reached efficiently and amicably.

The method consists of four key elements:

1. Separate the PEOPLE from the problem;

2. Focus on INTERESTS, not positions;

3. Invent OPTIONS for mutual gain;

4. Insist on objective CRITERIA.

A comparative assessment of the three approaches (soft, hard, and principled) may be seen in Figure 6.2.

---

[2]From *Getting To Yes* by Roger Fisher and William Ury. Copyright © 1981 by Roger Fisher and William Ury. Reprinted by permission of Houghton Mifflin Company.

Figure 6.2. Three Approaches To Negotiation[3]

PROBLEM Positional Bargaining: Which Game Should You Play?		SOLUTION Change the Game — Negotiate on the Merits
SOFT	HARD	PRINCIPLED
Participants are friends.	Participants are adversaries.	Participants are problem-solvers.
The goal is agreement.	The goal is victory.	The goal is a wise outcome reached efficiently and amicably.
Make concessions to cultivate the relationship.	Demand concessions as a condition of the relationship.	Separate the people from the problem.
Be soft on the people and the problem.	Be hard on the problem and the people.	Be soft on the people, hard on the problem.
Trust others.	Distrust others.	Proceed independent of trust.
Change your position easily.	Dig in to your position.	Focus on interests, not positions.
Make offers.	Make threats.	Explore interests.
Disclose your bottom line.	Mislead as to your bottom line.	Avoid having a bottom line.
Accept one-sided losses to reach agreement	Demand one-sided gains as the price of agreement.	Invent options for mutual gain.
Search for the single answer: the one *they* will accept.	Search for the single answer: the one *you* will accept.	Develop multiple options to choose from; decide later.
Insist on agreement.	Insist on your position.	Insist on objective criteria.
Try to avoid a contest of will.	Try to win a contest of will.	Try to reach a result based on standards independent of will.
Yield to pressure.	Apply pressure.	Reason and be open to reasons; yield to principle, not pressure.

---

[3]Fisher, R., and Ury, W., *op. cit.*, p. 13. Used with permission.

INPUT 2

A. Use of Questions

According to Nierenberg, questions may be used during negotiations to:

- draw attention

- get information

- give information

- make others think

- bring the others' thinking to a conclusion.

These are the *five functions* of questions.

A skilled negotiator should also know, as Nierenberg points out, how not to answer when questioned. This is possible when you:

- leave the other party with the assumption that he or she has been answered

- answer incompletely

- answer inaccurately

- leave the other person without the desire to pursue the questioning process further.

Karrass adds some useful hints from the standpoint of the questioner:

- it is generally wise to ask a question even if it appears to be a bit personal, or even ridiculous

- the purpose of a question is to find out about an opponent's values, assumptions, and intentions

- the detective's concept of interrogation appears inappropriate to negotiations and likely to be counter-productive

- it is best to keep questions simple (where, what, who, which, why, when, and how).

B. Listening and Responding

It seems that North Americans use the five listening and responding sytles in the following frequency: (1) evaluative, (2) interpretative, (3) supportive, (4) probing, and (5) understanding.

No style is in itself good or bad. It depends upon the people involved as well as as the situation they are in. However, it has been shown that:

(a) The overuse or underuse of any style can be a handicap when counseling other people:

(b) The failure to select the appropriate response explains many miscommunications;

(c) The understanding response can be quite powerful, especially at the outset of interaction;

(d) The avoidance of giving an evaluative response in the early stages of a relationship is indicated in most cases (a value judgement often leads to another value judgment);

The usefulness of the five styles can be roughly described as follows:

Understanding: helps the negotiator to expand upon his/her ideas, feelings, perceptions, etc., and increases the accuracy of communication between the parties involved.

Probing: helps to clarify the problem and assist the negotiator in exploring the full implications of his/her decision.

Supportive: is useful when the negotiator needs to feel accepted and is looking for support and reassurance.

Interpretative: helps the negotiator realize the impact of what he/she just said on the other party. This can lead to a constructive confrontation.

Evaluative: is useful when the "opponent" is specifically asked to make a value judgment, to disclose his/her own values, attitudes, and feelings.[4]

To improve your listening and responding skills, the following checklist may be useful:

• Speak only when necessary

• Look at things through others' eyes

• Show active interest — this convinces the other person that you are listening

• Summarize and paraphrase

• Focus attention on main points

• Be careful of your biases/prejudices

• Take notes

• Check understanding.

---

[4] Casse, P. *Training for the Cross-Cultural Mind.* Washington, D.C.: SIETAR. Second Edition, 1981, pp. 135-136.

INPUT 3

A. Individual Factors Affecting Negotiation

Figure 6.3. Basic Factors in Each Individual's Make-up Affecting the Negotiating Process

Self-Assessment Instrument

Self-Rating	Rating the Other Party

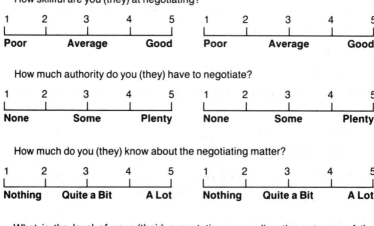

How skillful are you (they) at negotiating?

1	2	3	4	5		1	2	3	4	5
Poor		**Average**		**Good**		**Poor**		**Average**		**Good**

How much authority do you (they) have to negotiate?

1	2	3	4	5		1	2	3	4	5
None		**Some**		**Plenty**		**None**		**Some**		**Plenty**

How much do you (they) know about the negotiating matter?

1	2	3	4	5		1	2	3	4	5
Nothing	**Quite a Bit**		**A Lot**			**Nothing**	**Quite a Bit**		**A Lot**	

What is the level of your (their) expectations regarding the outcome of the negotiating?

1	2	3	4	5		1	2	3	4	5
Low		**Moderate**		**High**		**Low**		**Moderate**		**High**

Questions: 1. What training on *how to negotiate* do people receive in different cultures?

2. What are different cultural ways to define *power?*

3. Who is an *expert* in Japan, the U.S.A., Europe, Latin America?

4. How do people from various cultures express their aspirations?

B. Motivation and Negotiation

Preparation for negotiation includes some guesswork about the party one is to negotiate with. There is, of course, some danger in attaching too much importance to this strategic activity by changing the guesses into preconceived ideas or perceptions. Participants in the Workshop reflect upon two factors that have impact on the success (or failure) of any kind of negotiation:

Figure 6.4. Motivations And Needs[5]

Definitions: 1. **Need for Achievement:** These negotiators are eager to perform well, achieve the goals, improve, be more effective, get involved in challenging situations, be on their own, get feedback, take responsibility for the decisions made, and take moderate risks.

2. **Need for Affiliation:** These negotiators like to interact with others. Enjoy the exchange of ideas between different people, teamwork, and synergy. They are sensitive to

[5]This model is related to Dr. D. McClelland's theory on motivation.

others' needs and expectations. Negotiation is based on cooperation and to achieve a win/win objective is what the negotiators aim for.

3. **Need for Power:** These negotiators like power either for its own sake or for the benefit of the team and organizations they represent. They like to influence or have an impact on others. They enjoy prestigious activities and are highly sensitive to status and formal recognition.

Questions:

1. Can you identify cultures in which the dominant needs are achievement, affiliation, or power?

2. What happens when people from different cultures and needs meet to negotiate? Document your diagnosis with illustrations.

3. How can you recognize — in behavioral terms — that a negotiator is power, affiliation, or achievement oriented?

C. *Communication and Negotiation*

Figure 6.5. Communication Orientations[6]

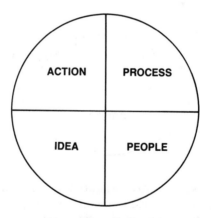

Definitions:

1. **Action oriented negotiators** are interested in objectives, results, doing, achieving, getting things done, moving ahead, accomplishing, being efficient.

2. **Process oriented negotiators** concentrate on organizations, structures, processes, facts, strategies, tactics, options, methods.

---

[6]Casse, P., *Training for the Cross-Cultural Mind.* Washington, D.C.: SIETAR, 1981, pp. 125-132.

3. **People oriented negotiators** like to approach negotiations through teamwork, sound communications, good relations, social interactions.

4. **Idea oriented negotiators** focus upon concepts, theories, models, abstracts, intellectual constructions, emotion, creativity.

Questions: 1. How do you meet the basic expectations of a negotiator who belongs to a highly process oriented culture? Which strategy would you use?

2. Is it true that:

   (a)   action oriented negotiators can be perceived as **impulsive** and **dangerous**?

   (b)   process oriented negotiators can be seen as being slow at making decisions and **lacking imagination**?

   (c)   people oriented negotiators seem to pay too much attention to the relationships and **forget** the purpose of the negotiation?

   (d)   idea oriented negotiators sometimes behave like **dreamers** and **unrealistic people**?

3. Which countries in the world have (or had):

   • **Action** as the dominant orientation?

   • **Process** as the dominant orientation?

   • **People** as the dominant orientation?

   • **Ideas** as the dominant orientation?

6. Readings:

1. Deal, T.E., and Kennedy, A.A. *Corporate Cultures*. Reading, MA: Addison-Wesley, 1982.

2. Kennedy, G., Benson, J., and McMillan, J. *Managing Negotiations*. Englewood Cliffs, NJ: Prentice-Hall, Inc., 1982.

3. Nierenberg, G.I., *Creative Business Negotiating*. New York: Hawthorn Books, Inc., 1971.

CHAPTER 7
Non-Verbal Communication and Negotiation

"When you try to examine somebody consciously by overpowering him, it elicits from him the response of resisting you. There are some people who don't resist being overpowered, but who go into a trance. However, neither resistance nor cooperation is a demonstration of anything except the ability of people to respond. Everybody who is living can respond. The questions are: how and to what? Your job when you do hypnosis is to notice what people respond to naturally."

J. Grinder and R. Bandler

In negotiation, what is *not* said is in many cases more important than what is openly expressed by the parties involved. Effective negotiators are particularly good at controlling (consciously or unconsciously) their body language and at the same time adjusting to the many non-verbal signals they receive from the opposite negotiator(s).

Some people believe that it is possible to "read a person like a book." We beg to disagree. People are not books. Besides, gestures and body postures that have a meaning in a certain culture can have a completely different significance in a different cultural environment. We do not know for sure what gestures mean. The only thing we know is that they mean something. The meaning of any non-verbal communication act depends upon:

(1) the individual involved;

(2) the context in which the act is performed; and

(3) the cultural background of the interacting people.

What fascinates us is the tremendous impact of the "silent language" on the negotiation process. Everything counts during the negotiation: the time of the negotiation (morning, lunch time, late in the evening) the table (round, square), the lights (white, in the middle of the room), the use of microphones, the breaks, the phone calls, the space between the chairs, the way the negotiators dress, and so on. Everything is important. We have personally reached the conclusion that effective negotiators are fully aware of the existence of all these factors and that they are able to use them to their advantage.

Watching negotiators in action, we have been amazed many times by their subtle way of responding to the various elements of what we call the *nego-*

tiating vortex. They are in and at the same time they are out. They are aware and yet they follow their intuition. They push and pull. They are highly flexible. Without knowing it, they are very good at using *hypnosis* to alter the other party's state of consciousness.

Workshop 7

1. Aim: To become more aware of the importance of non-verbal communication in negotiation.

2. Objectives: Participants will:

(1) Review some of the key aspects of the non-verbal communication process;

(2) Analyze the impact of non-verbal communication in negotiation;

(3) Learn how to use *hypnosis* to improve their negotiating capability.

3. Process:

First Exercise. This exercise is used to demonstrate Chomsky's[1] assertion that people who communicate keep shifting from a deep structure to a surface structure in:

(1) *Deleting* or *omitting* some elements of the message that has been sent;

(2) *Adding* some new information to the original message or stimulus;

(3) *Distorting* or *changing* the meanings of some parts of the intended message.

The exercise has four parts:

Phase I   A picture (opposite page) is shown to the group (for 2 or 3 minutes) and then taken away. Participants have to describe what the picture is all about. They are asked to do so as accurately as possible. (They normally forget to mention some elements, add a few, and distort the meaning of some of the features of the picture.)

---

[1]Chomsky, Noam. *Problems of Knowledge and Freedom,* N.Y.: Vintage Books, 1971.

Phase 2. The facilitator whispers a sentence to one participant who has to repeat it to the person next to him or her and so on until the last participant who has to share it aloud with the group. The group members compare the first statement with the last one.

The sentence is: *"Pure communication is not impossible but very difficult."*

Phase 3. The facilitator — without saying anything — shakes hands *in a very loose way* with one of the participants. The participant is asked to share his or her impressions with the group which then analyzes the various cultural assumptions related to a loose handshake.

Loose Handshaking*

Culture X	Culture Y
1. Not honest	1. Introvert
2. Weak personality	2. Shy
3. _____	3. _____
4. _____	4. _____
5. _____	5. _____

* to be completed by the group.

Phase 4. The group examines a list of non-verbal signals, their potential cultural meanings, as well as their impact on the negotiating process:

Figure 7.1 Non-Verbal Signals and Negotiation

Non-Verbal Signals	Potential Cultural Meanings	Impact on Negotiation
1. Facial Expression	It could mean the person is:	This non-verbal signal can lead to:
— frowning	— doubtful or	— defensiveness
— smiling	— sarcastic or	— emotional reactions
— staring	— arrogant or	— anger
Others *	. . . .	. . . .
. . . .	. . . .	. . . .
. . . .	. . . .	. . . .
2. Gestures		
— pointing	— talking down or	— resistance
— banging	— angry or	— fight
— clenching fists	— defiant or	— breakdown
Others *	. . . .	. . . .
. . . .	. . . .	. . . .
. . . .	. . . .	. . . .
3. Tone of Voice		
— low pitch	— self-assured or	— mistrust
— high pitch	— emotional or	— withdrawal
— very low tone	— secretive or	— attention
Others *	. . . .	. . . .
. . . .	. . . .	. . . .
. . . .	. . . .	. . . .
4. Sitting		
— sitting on edge of chair	— nervous or	— tension
— crossing leg	— defensive or	— new arguments
— balancing foot	— irritated or	— counter argument
Others *	. . . .	. . . .
. . . .	. . . .	. . . .
. . . .	. . . .	. . . .
5. Others *	. . . .	. . . .
. . . .	. . . .	. . . .
. . . .	. . . .	. . . .

* to be added by the group.

Second Exercise. **(A)** A series of short exercises are used to pinpoint cultural differences in perceptions: Participants look at the picture *"A Negotiation in Progress"* and: (1) pinpoint some of the key non-verbal clues expressed by the characters; (2) analyze them from a cross-cultural perspective (how would they interpret the various clues if they were Japanese, Latin Americans, North Americans, Africans?).

A Negotiation in Progress[2]

(B) The group looks at the sketch below[3] and is asked to describe what they have just seen in a completely neutral way (the face of a man). After a while, they freely express their feelings and subjective impressions connected with the drawing.

---

[2]World Bank Photo.

[3]Drawing by Olivier Casse.

A discussion follows on:

1. The impact of *prejudices* on negotiation;

2. The importance of *first impressions* when we meet someone for negotiation;

3. The sources of prejudices in intercultural relations.

(C) A simulated negotiation on *"In Favor or Against Abortion"*[4] is organized using the fish bowl approach (six people in the middle of the room, three in favor and three against).

Each negotiator has reviewed some confidential instructions. He or she must follow them during the negotiation. It is up to the observers to identify the behaviors that the negotiators are following.

Confidential Instructions for the Negotiators

Team 1	Negotiator 1.	Expresses anger non-verbally;
	Negotiator 2.	Shows sadness non-verbally;
	Negotiator 3.	Demonstrates frustration non-verbally.
Team 2	Negotiator 4.	Shares sympathy and positive feelings non-verbally;
	Negotiator 5.	Expresses agreement and support non-verbally;
	Negotiator 6.	Shows confidence and assurance non-verbally.

The performance of the negotiators is discussed during a debriefing session.

(D) Each member of the group gets a set of three pictures and fills out (independently) the gestures tally sheet, Figure 7.2 (20 minutes).

---

[4]Cultural reactions to the topic (abortion) selected for the exercise can be first identified and analyzed by the group.

Picture 1[5]

Picture 2

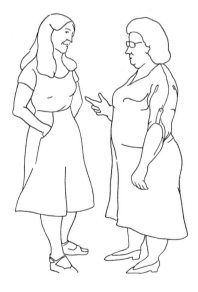

Picture 3

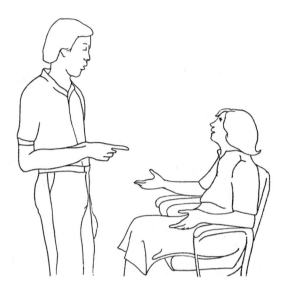

Figure 7.2 Gestures Tally Sheet

Cultural Perceptions   **Cultural Reactions**

For each picture, give 3 different cultural interpretations of what is happening.	Explain what your reactions are. (What are the cultural values, beliefs, and assumptions that underlie your reactions?)
Picture 1	
Picture 2	
Picture 3	

Participants meet in threes and share their cultural perceptions and reactions (30 minutes).

(E) A Critical Incident

Each participant looks at the picture above and answers the following question in writing:

"Assuming that something dramatic has just happened and that you are responsible for it, what kind of non-verbal reactions could you have to make sure that the people around you are going to calm down?"

(F) The group analyzes five critical non-verbal signals (and their cultural variations) that are used in negotiations:[6]

1. The yes/no signals;
2. Contradictory signals;
3. Overkill signals;
4. Barrier signals;
5. Threat signals.

---

[6]Morris, D. *Manwatching. A Field Guide to Human Behavior.* New York: Harry N. Abrams, Inc., 1977.

1. The Yes/No Signals

Cultural Ways to Express Yes and No Non-Verbally	
YES	**NO**
1. The head moves vertically up and down (one or several times).	1. The head moves horizontally from side to side.
2. The head tilts (as a pendulum) from side to side.	2. The head turns to one side and back.
3. The forefinger moves up and down.	3. The forefinger moves position laterally.
Others:*	Others* ....

* to be added by the group.

2. The Contradictory Signals

Different Cultural Ways to Express Contradictory Signals
1. Smiling and perspiring at the same time.
2. Well controlled gestures and fast breathing.
3. Nodding as if listening and foot tapping.
4. Low pitch of the voice and smiling.
5. Attending with eyes and body sagging.
6. Frowning and nodding yes.
7. Bold stare and head down.
8. Forceful statement and hands in pockets.
Others:* ....

* to be completed by the group.

3. The Overkill Signals

What do you think of the following behavior:

1. Someone who laughs "too loud" and "too long";
2. People who sit with their legs wide open;
3. A person who shakes hands forever?

The group examines some key non-verbal differences between *demonstrative* and *reserved* cultures.

4. The Barrier Signals

Some non-verbal signals can be used as protective devices such as:

1. Hiding behind somebody else;

2. Putting a piece of furniture between oneself and the other person;

3. Looking elsewhere and avoiding eye contact;

4. Covering up the face with a hand or other objects (e.g., book, pen);

5. Giggling;

6. Crossing hands and arms in front of the body;

7. Crossing legs when sitting;

8. Turning one's back to someone;

9. Rubbing hands together.

Others (barrier signals used in other cultures);

_____

_____

_____

_____

5. The Threat Signals

Participants analyze the following threat signals from a cross-cultural perspective. (Do these signals exist in your culture? Do you use other signals? How would you interpret the signals?)[7]

1. The fist shake;	5. The eye stab;
2. The hand chop;	6. The self-choke;
3. The neck wring;	7. The self-bite;
4. The neck choke;	8. The throat slit.

---

[7]Morris, D., *Manwatching. A Field Guide to Human Behavior.* New York: Harry N. Abrams, Inc., 1977. Drawings by Priscilla Barrett from page 196 are used with permission of Equinox (Oxford) Ltd.

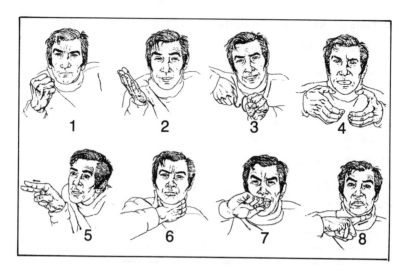

(G) The analysis of "non-verbal leakage" — it is vital for negotiators to be aware of clues that give information away without their consent. The participants meet in threes and answer the following question:

According to you, what kind of information can people give away through the following clues:

Clues	Cultural Interpretation of Potential Information Given Away*
1. Shaky hands	
2. Crossing and uncrossing legs	
3. Playing with spectacles	
4. Covering mouth with one hand	
5. Stroking chin	
6. Touching nose	
7. Scratching head	
8. Pressing lips	
Others* _____	
_____	

* to be completed by the participants

(H) Group members are organized in threes with a performer, a responder, and an observer (they rotate so that each member has an opportunity to perform the three roles) and discuss three topics given by the trainer and using the observer tally sheet (Figure 7.3) to analyze the non-verbal clues given by the performer during the exercise.

Topics for Discussion: (5 minutes each)

1. Talk about how Japanese people express themselves non-verbally;

2. Identify at least three typical non-verbal clues used by Latin American people;

3. Describe the main characteristics of the North American non-verbal language.

Figure 7.3 Observer Tally Sheet

	Round 1	Round 2	Round 3
Eye Contact			
Body posture			
Vocal intonation			
Use of space			
Handling of time			

Third Exercise. The group is introduced to the Neuro-Linguistic Programming (NLP) approach and its implications for negotiation.

Several years ago Richard Bandler and John Grinder began studying the communication behaviors of psychotherapists widely recognized for their therapeutic successes. Their aim was to identify patterns of behavior associated with effective results, to codify these patterns, and to make them available to others who aspired to be effective therapists. They chose as their basic subjects Virginia Satir, a family therapist, and Milton Erickson, a clinical hypnotist; another subject of more indirect analysis was Fritz Perls, with whom Grinder studied. The skills and behaviors identified were referred to as "magic," a traditional term for any process that people do not understand. In reality, once people learn these patterns of behavior, they, too, can be "magicians."

Bandler and Grinder note that their background is that of linguists with a focus on the process of communication rather than the content. The core of their theory is their interpretation of the ways in which linguistic meanings are mentally assigned to basic thoughts and experiences. This interpretation, called the Meta Model, serves as the foundation of their secondary model of interpersonal communication effectiveness, which is known simply as the Communication Model. Although the communication methods proposed by Bandler and Grinder in accordance with these models were developed to improve communication effectiveness in the context of therapy, they can also be used to advantage in business and industry and in group facilitation.[8]

Several learning modules are proposed to the participants so that they can experience the NLP model:

First Module

Participants meet in threes. Each member of the team (one at a time) has to think about: (a) something that gave him/her great pleasure in the past; and (b) an event that triggered great displeasure. They do not say anything. They just signal that they have identified the event (also one at a time) raising their right hand. It is up to the two other members of the team to watch the non-verbal signals (color of the skin, breathing, tension of the muscles, lips, etc.), and guess, each time, if the event was good or bad. When the exercise is over, they talk about:

a. Their ability to read subtle non-verbal signals;

b. The implications for negotiation;

c. The cultural differences that exist regarding the non-verbal expression of feelings and emotions.

Second Module

The same groups of three organize themselves so that one plays the role of a performer, one the role of a responder, and one the role of an observer. When ready, the performers are asked to leave the room for a couple of minutes.

The responders are informed that when the performers come back into the room they will have to talk about a given topic ("Effective Negotiation is Based on Hypnosis") for three minutes. The responders are instructed to face or match (in a subtle but systematic way) all the gestures and body postures of the performers when making sure that the conversation is alive and interesting. The observers watch (do not intervene at all) and prepare their comments for when the exercise is over. The discussion that follows should cover:

a. Was the performer aware of what was happening?

b. What about the impact of the "matching behavior" on the interaction?

c. Is this used in negotiations?

---

[8]Reprinted from: J. William Pfeiffer and Leonard D. Goodstein, Editors. *The 1982 Annual for Facilitators, Trainers, and Consultants,* San Diego, CA. Copyright 1982, University Associates, Inc. Used with permission.

Third Module

One member of the group leaves the room. The two other team members are asked to watch (very carefully) the eye movements of the third participant when he/she comes back and is requested to answer a series of questions. They should take notes of the *very first reactions of the eyes* without disclosing what they are doing. They should also make sure that they sit right in front of the performer:

Question 1: Can you please describe the house where you were born?

Question 2: Imagine the ideal place in the world where you would like to live. Can you describe it?

Question 3: Summarize the last conversation you had with your boss. What did he/she say?

Question 4: You meet with "God." What do you say?

Question 5: Describe your feelings when you are very happy. What are they?

The debriefing of this exercise consists of explaining that people use three "representational systems" to understand (or give meaning) to the world: visual, auditory, and kinesthetic. Each individual has a preferred system that he or she uses more often. The system that a person feels more comfortable with can be identified (according to the NLP approach) through the eye movements.

Here are the three primary representational systems (see Conceptual Framework: Input 3):

(1) People who are *visual* use words like see, look, focus, picture. Their eyes have a tendency to look upward (left if it is past related [Question 1] and right if it is future.)

(2) People who are *auditory* use words like hear, sound, listen, tune in. They look to the left (remembered auditory: Question 3) and to the right (constructed auditory: Question 4). They also look down and to the left (internal dialogue).

(3) People who are *kinesthetic* use words like feel, touch, reach, handle. The typical eye movement is downward and to the right (Question 5).

After a brief discussion on what happened during the exercise, the trainer asks the group to react to the three following questions:

• Assuming that you negotiate with someone, how do you identify his or her primary representational system?

• Now that you know what it is, what do you do?

• If your eyes go up to the right, what does it mean?

3. Time: At least one full day.

4. Conceptual Framework:

INPUT 1

Non-Verbal Communication

We get important signals non-verbally. A skilled negotiator must learn to understand hidden or body language, which has a very powerful impact on the total communication process. Mel Schnaper in an article published in the *Bridge*[9] mentioned five important dimensions of body language:

- Body movements of all sorts, including facial gestures, hand motions, leg movements, and shifts in overall body posture, i.e., Kinesics.

- Interpersonal space — how close or distant individuals stand from each other, i.e., Proxemics.

- The silence between verbal exchanges in conversations, i.e., Chronemics.

- Eye contact or avoidance, i.e., Oculescis.

- Body contact such as handshake, embrace, or pat on the shoulder, i.e., Haptics.

INPUT 2

Meta Communication and Negotiation

Meta communication relates to the hidden meanings of what we send and receive. According to Nierenberg,[10] negotiators should know that:

1. What we say first is more important.

2. The use of personal pronouns is revealing of the position of the speaker on the topic at hand (I and we mean more commitment than they, he, she. They often announce some kind of prejudice).

3. Expressions like "people think," "we," "experts in the field," "in my humble opinion," are screens that can hide arrogance and false modesty.

4. A "yes" followed by a "but" generally announces an attack or a killing.

5. Skillful negotiators use expressions like "I think you'll like what I'm about to say" (some good news is coming up), "it goes without say-

---

[9]Schnapper, M. "International Sales Skills," *The Bridge,* Volume 6, Number 2, Summer 1981, pp. 30-33.

[10]META-TALK, Copyright 1973 by Gerald I. Nierenberg and Henry H. Calaro. Reprinted with permission by Simon & Schuster, Inc.

ing" (you must agree on this one), "off the top of my head" (I share with you what I think right now, without any preparation), "would you be kind enough to . . ." (I need your help), "I am sure that someone as intelligent as you" (a big stroke on the other party's ego). All the above expressions are used as *softeners.*

6. Negotiators also try to put the people they negotiate with in a negative frame of mind in using *foreboders* such as "nothing is wrong" (there is something wrong for sure), "it really does not matter" (it does, of course).

7. The following statements are used to arouse the negotiator's interest: "and do you know what he did?" "Guess what he decided?", "You are not going to believe this."

8. Key words such as "go on," "excellent," "I like it," "and then" are incentives to keep the other party talking.

9. Negotiators who want *to put down* the other party use expressions like: "are you happy now?", "don't make me laugh," "don't be ridiculous," "needless to say."

10. What is important in negotiation is not so much what the speaker is saying or what he/she thinks he/she is saying, but what the other party thinks the speaker is saying.

INPUT 3

Representational Systems and Eye Movements

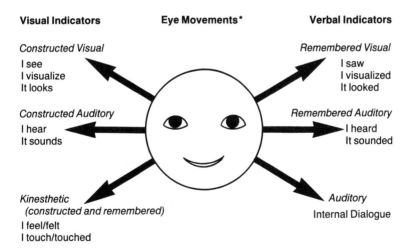

Visual Indicators	Eye Movements*	Verbal Indicators

Constructed Visual
I see
I visualize
It looks

Remembered Visual
I saw
I visualized
It looked

Constructed Auditory
I hear
It sounds

Remembered Auditory
I heard
It sounded

Kinesthetic
 (constructed and remembered)
I feel/felt
I touch/touched

Auditory
Internal Dialogue

* All the eye movements are reversed for left handed people.

INPUT 1

Hypnosis and Negotiation

The following two statements by Bandler and Grinder emphasize the relationship between hypnosis and negotiation.

One: "We need only three things to be an absolutely exquisite communicator . . . The first one is to know what outcome you want. The second is that you need flexibility in your behavior. You need to be able to generate lots and lots of different behaviors to find out what responses you get. The third is you need to have enough sensory experience to notice when you get the responses that you want."

Two: "Hypnosis is a very natural process . . . (it) is only a word that describes the tools that you use to systematically take someone into an altered state of consciousness."

The following hypnotic tools can be used (or are used) by negotiators who want to get the other party in an altered state of consciousness:

1. Ask the other party to describe to you an event that they were involved in and that had such an impact on them that they were not aware of anything else at the time of the incident (in doing so, the other party will go back to what happened in the past, experience it once more, and go into "trance");

2. Use statements that can be immediately *verified* by the other party (that gives you credibility) and then connect them with leading statements ("it is quite warm in this room," and "I wonder if . . .") which are not — or are less — verifiable;

3. Use smooth transitions when negotiating (use words like and, as, while, because, when);

4. Incorporate what the other party says or experiences into your argument;

5. Offer alternatives;

6. Use body mirroring;

7. Describe to the other party an intense, commonly-shared trance state (the other party will try to follow you and in doing so will get into trance);

8. "Anchor" or use part of a past experience to bring back the entire experience;

9. Mark out some words non-verbally when talking;

10. Use tag questions (or add a negation at the end of a sentence: it is alright, isn't it?);

11. Do or say something unexpected (the other party will then be "on hold" and then offer some clear suggestions);

12. Overload the other party's conscious in asking him or her to pay attention to what he or she is experiencing at that time of the negotiation;

13. Be congruent in your expectations and use straight personal power; use quotes;

14. Stack realities in telling stories within stories (the other party will have some difficulty keeping track of what has been covered);

15. Stay out of the content, mention the obvious, and connect with the response you want to elicit;

16. Use the "illusion of choice" (Erickson) in presenting false alternatives ("do you prefer this, or this?");

17. Build on resistance. Do not push or pull;

18. Ask the other party to pretend;

19. Use generalizations as well as extrapolations.

Reflect upon the following:[11]

- Your job when you do hypnosis is to notice what people respond to naturally;

- Hypnosis is not a process of taking control of people. It is a process of giving them control of themselves by providing feedback that they would not ordinarily have;

- Trance is only taking your conscious experience and altering it to something else;

- In the context of hypnosis, you do not go fast by going quickly. You go fast by going slowly;

- The meaning of any communication — not just in hypnosis but in life — is not what you think it means; it is the response it elicits;

- Hypnosis is a process of amplification;

- Hypnosis is only a way of expediting change;

- Generally people are convinced that they are in a trance when they experience something very different from their normal state. One person's normal state may be another person's trance.

---

[11]Bandler, R., and Grinder, J. *Frogs into Princes*. Moab, Ut: Real People Press, 1979.

6. Readings

1. Bandler, R., and Grinder, J. *Trance-Formations. Neuro-Linguistic Programming and the Structure of Hypnosis.* Moab, Ut: Real People Press, 1981.

2. LeCron, L. M. *The Complete Guide to Hypnosis.* New York: Harper & Row, 1971.

3. Morris, D. *Manwatching. A Field Guide to Human Behavior.* New York: Harry N. Abrams, Inc., 1977.

CHAPTER 8
A Gestalt Orientation to Intercultural Negotiations

"Be
As you are
And so see
Who you are
and how you are
Let go
For a moment or two
of what you ought to do
And discover what you do do
Risk a little if you can
Feel your own feelings
Say your own words
Think your own thoughts
Be your own self
Discover
Let the plan for you
Grow from within you."

F. Perls

Negotiation is not a "game" and we do not have to play "roles". It is a natural way of responding to the external realities of one's life. You interact with others all the time. Yet there are no "set" rules that you have to follow. You create your own rules and guidelines. No one knows your needs more than you do. And if you are your "true" self ("authentic"), you will soon discover the most efficient way to satisfy your needs. This is the essence of the Gestalt approach or orientation. There are at least six assumptions that are significant for intercultural negotiations.

- You are responsible for finding your own path; be responsible for what you say and do.

- You don't make concessions in order to please or win others over.

- The secret of success in life, if any, is to control your present ("here and now") and not to worry about the past and the future.

- Going out of your way to avoid conflict or dissensions is running away from reality. Conflict is, and shall remain, an essential part of your being. This polarity of negative and positive forces is at the heart of the creative act. Like varying shades in the petals of flowers, your uniqueness lies in being different while sharing the same dominant "color."

- Being able to say "no," when you should really say "no," is not only an act of courage and a show of self-confidence, but a true self-expression. You are an autonomous being; so are others.

- Learning to expand and enrich one's internal reservoir of reactive and proactive competence (to know where you are and what you want) is the key to success.

Some quick reactions come to our mind. How do you *negotiate* when:

- You follow no set rules;

- You aggressively pursue your own self-interest;

- You do not try to resolve conflicts;

- You listen to no one except your own inner voice;

- You try to get away with hurt feelings and bruised egos; and

- You withdraw from time to time to regain "energy"?

The following Workshop seeks to answer some of these questions.

Workshop 8

1. Aim: To understand the Gestalt way of looking at intercultural negotiations.

2. Objective: Participants will:

(1) Examine the significance of the Gestalt approach in intercultural negotiations;

(2) Assess some of their negotiating attitudes from a Gestalt perspective;

(3) Analyze Gestalt orientation in its effective and ineffective dimensions.

3. Process:

First Exercise. Participants go through the following exercise in three stages.

Stage 1: Each participant fills out blanks in the exercise, working individually.

Stage 2: Each participant chooses a partner to share three reasons "why this is true of me." And another three reasons to prove "why it is not so."

Stage 3: The trainer discusses the following questions with the whole group:

- What is the "cost" of being authentic in intercultural negotiations?

- What do I do when things do not work out well for me?

- What is the cultural dimension of the exercise?

Being Your Own Self

Fill in all blanks. A straight line means that you have to insert one word/figure. A broken line means that you may choose to insert one or more words.

"My name is .... I am_____years of age. I am_____by profession and very proud of being so. My parents made me what I am by ....
I have varied interests such as _____, _____, and_____. Three things which appeal to me most are _____, _____ and_____. I am very polite but frankly I cannot stand _____, _____, and_____. I do not play roles; I am _____ and I expect every other person to be so. If I like something, I respond positively. If not, I withdraw. People may call this_____ or _____. I don't care. I am not a Messiah parading this earth to wipe every tear and liberate every damned soul. I am an ordinary human and would like to stay that way. In my organization people are generally_____ and _____. I respond to the reality surrounding me. I face problems by acting the way I do, but in retrospect I do not regret it. There is time to be nice and decent; but sometimes one has to assert oneself and blow up the mask of hypocrisy that tends to vitiate the true meaning and purpose of life.

When I meet with other people to discuss important matters, my opening statement is ....
I share my_____. What others say and do affects me deeply. I use my imagination and intuition to interpret the meaning of these responses. And once I am back, I react. These reactions are sometimes_____. I do not carry a sense of guilt about anything, I do not let the cultural environment bother me to behave differently. Nor do I agree with others without reason. _____ or _____, my feelings are my own. And I give you and everyone else the same right. We can negotiate better if we remain our true selves."

Second Exercise. People with a Gestalt orientation do not believe that there is a set of rules that govern or guide their behavior. They flow with the tide and enjoy being what they are. Yet there are clearly *effective* and *ineffective* dimensions of this orientation. The following table (Figure 8.1) explains these variations. The trainer may share these ideas with the group and ask participants to identify these distinctions in terms of their own negotiating styles.

Figure 8.1 Authentic Management and Intercultural Negotiations

Effective Dimension	Ineffective Dimension
1. Keeping firm grip on the content and the process, yet keeping oneself flexible (afloat).	1. Being firm and rigid; inability to change and to adjust.
2. Using conflict situations to come up with creative solutions.	2. Arriving at deadlocks because of unresolved conflicts.
3. Communicating on the basis of internal feedback as a true expression of one's own self and not deliberately hurting someone.	3. Communicating one's thoughts and feelings without regard for their impact on others.
4. Being able to say "no" in a non-threatening way.	4. Saying "no" and closing the door.
5. Withdrawing from time to time to think, evaluate, and regain energy.	5. Withdrawing and losing contact.
6. Being able to see the *whole* and part of a situation.	6. Getting preoccupied with trivia and not seeing the whole.
7. Enhancing internal competence in a *positive* way.	7. Increasing competence in a *negative* way.
8. Combining intuition with intellect.	8. Being intuitive without being strong on intellect.
9. Being serious and playful; switching.	9. Projecting a dull profile; always sharing dullness.
10. Building genuine and warm relationships.	10. Being authentic but always showing lack of concern for others.

Third Exercise. Members of the group go through the following self-assessment exercise that has been designed to help them identify and analyze the attitudes that have a strong impact on how people negotiate.

Self-Assessment Exercise on Negotiating Attitudes
(A Gestalt Approach)

Circle the appropriate score for each item:

| | ---Scores--- | | |
When negotiating I:	Marginally	Somewhat	Very Much
1. Try to avoid risk	1	3	5
2. Like to know where I am going	1	3	5
3. Give up too easily when faced with obstacles	1	3	5
4. Avoid discussion on subjects that I do not master	1	3	5
5. Have a tendency to settle for less than I could have claimed	1	3	5
6. Try to avoid confrontations as much as possible	1	3	5
7. Draw back when the risk is too high	1	3	5
8. Withdraw under attack	1	3	5
9. Look for clarifications	1	3	5
10. Am apologetic	1	3	5
11. Avoid ambiguity as much as possible	1	3	5
12. Take calculated risks	1	3	5
13. Follow my pre-negotiating plan	1	3	5
14. Take a safe stance	1	3	5
15. Resent being pushed around	1	3	5

Negotiating Attitudes — Score Sheet

For each item report the score you selected: 1 for "marginally," 3 for "somewhat," and 5 for "very much". The total cannot be below 5 and above 15. The grand total should be between 15 and 75.

Attitude 1.

Items	1	5	7	10	14
Scores	( ) +	( ) +	( ) +	( ) +	( ) = _____

Attitude 2.

Items	3	6	8	12	15
Scores	( ) +	( ) +	( ) +	( ) +	( ) = _____

Attitude 3.

Items	2	4	9	11	13
Scores	( ) +	( ) +	( ) +	( ) +	( ) = _____

Participants analyze their scores using the following descriptions of the three attitudes. They then work in small groups (four to six) on the three questions raised after the descriptions.

A. Descriptions of the Three Attitudes:

Attitude 1: Fear of *failure*. Some negotiators are not as effective as they could be because they are afraid of failing.

A score between 5 and 8 could mean that the fear is well under control; between 9 and 12 that the fear of failing could be a handicap to effective negotiation; between 13 and 15 that the fear is somewhat overwhelming.

Attitude 2: Fear of the *pain*. Some negotiators are reluctant to be involved in any kind of confrontation that can make them suffer.

A score between 5 and 8 could mean that the negotiator controls that fear very well; between 9 and 12 that some pain can be taken; between 13 and 15 that the fear to experience pain restricts the negotiator in his or her behavior.

Attitude 3: Fear of the *unknown*. Some negotiators do not feel safe when exploring new ground. A score between 5 and 8 could mean that the negotiator has no problem with the unknown; between 9 and 12 the unknown can be perceived as risky and trigger an avoidance reaction; between 13 and 15 that the fear of the unknown is such that the negotiator does not feel free to explore new options, possibilities, and opportunities.

B. Three Questions:

(a) What is the impact of the three fears on the way people negotiate?

(b) How are the three fears experienced in different cultures?

(c) What would you suggest to people who want to overcome the three fears?

4. Time: About 3 hours.

5. Conceptual Framework:

INPUT 1

The Shadow of Intercultural Negotiation

"The concept of the Shadow is used in the psychology of C.G. Jung to characterize those aspects of an individual's personality that he has not integrated into his self-image. The Shadow often contains characteristics that seem negative, alien, and threatening to the individual, and he frequently rejects them. In so doing, he denies part of himself. He is incomplete and unbalanced, using important life energy in an internal struggle against himself. Since the struggle to repress the Shadow can never be completely successful, he is also troubled by its intermittent appearance in his behavior."

S.M. Herman

Figure 8.2 Shadows and Negotiation

The Shadow of Intercultural Negotiation	
Western Negotiators*	**Eastern Negotiators***
1. Have complete trust	1. Distrust
2. Are open and share	2. Conceal ideas and cheat
3. Always look for a win-win situations	3. Accept win-lose situations
4. Rely on the negotiating team's strengths	4. Rely on the individual's stengths instead of the team's strengths
5. Are sensitive to the other party's needs	5. Are aggressive

*These are, of course, stereotypes.

INPUT 2

Contrasts between the Human Relations and
Gestalt Approaches Toward Negotiation

Human Relations	Gestalt
1. Team approach (resources that exist in the negotiating team are fully tapped). The team is in charge, not its members.	1. Full use of the individual strengths. Members of the negotiating team are entitled (even encouraged) to take personal initiatives.
2. Be considerate to the other party. Respect the people of the other team. Be sensitive.	2. Do not hesitate to push and be assertive. The members of the other team are also strong.
3. Negotiate on the basis of mutual understanding and cooperation.	3. Negotiate on the basis of strength and power.
4. When you negotiate, focus on all the members of the other team.	4. When you negotiate, focus on the weakest members of the other team.
5. Emphasis should be put on the "whys" of the negotiation.	5. Emphasis should be put on the "hows" of the negotiation.
6. Analyze problems when they occur. Process negotiating deadlocks.	6. Do not spend too much time on problems. If stuck, switch to another issue.
7. Confrontations and conflicts should be avoided or at least controlled so that they do not jeopardize the success of the negotiation.	7. Conflicts and confrontations are valued as being essential to synergy and creativity.
8. Competition within the team and between negotiators is reduced as much as possible.	8. Competition is perceived as healthy.
9. Be careful with your emotions and feelings.	9. Freely express your emotions and feelings.
10. Be low key. Do not dramatize.	10. Exaggerate and dramatize.
11. Pay attention to the other party's reactions (external feedback).	11. Pay attention to your own internal feedback.
12. Value interdependence.	12. Value autonomy and independence.

13. Believe in trust and openness.	13. Believe in being up-front.
14. Be neutral at times. Put things into perspective.	14. Be actively involved.
15. Understand and control.	15. Be involved and react spontaneously.

INPUT 3

Polarities and Conflicts in Negotiation

All individuals, whatever their cultural backgrounds are, have in themselves the opposites of their qualities or shortcomings. The following figure illustrates the "multilarity" of opposites related to the negotiating process:

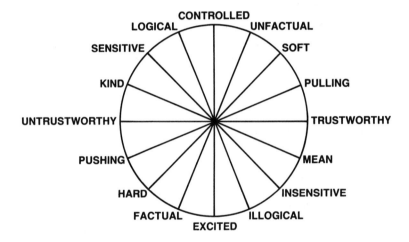

Polarities and Conflicts

Conflicts occur during negotiation when:

1. One of the negotiators projects one part of himself or herself onto someone else (In that case the fight is against oneself);

2. A negotiator has a quality that is very nice and at the same time frightening for the other party (I like what he has but I cannot have it, so I'll fight);

3. People are too self-demanding (I am hard on myself, so I am hard on others).

INPUT 4

Fixations and Negotiation

O. Ichazo,[1] the founder of *Arica,* has identified nine fixations that we find helpful in analyzing the problems that befall a negotiator regardless of his or her cultural background. The fixations are:

1. **Over-Perfectionist**

   The negotiator believes that everything needs to be improved-always. Nothing is ever good enough. He/she is over-critical of the external as well as internal (over self-critical) worlds.

2. **Over-Independent**

   The negotiator resents any kind of pressure advice. He/she wants to be free to make his/her own decisions.

3. **Over-Efficient**

   The negotiator is extremely extroverted. He/she always thinks in terms of changing (for the best, of course) the world. He/she is over-acting. He/She is never at rest and overdoes everything.

4. **Over-Reasoner**

   The negotiator has questions for everything. He/she never stops trying to understand. He/she believes that there is an answer to all questions. He/She is over-analytical.

5. **Over-Observant**

   The negotiator uses the "wait and see" approach all the time. He/she is not involved until he/she knows that he/she understands for sure what is going on. Aware of everything, he/she is on the sidelines almost constantly.

6. **Over-Adventurer**

   The negotiator is a risk taker. He/she wants action and enjoys discovery. He/She cannot resist the temptation of an adventure. Everything new and mysterious appeals to him/her.

7. **Over-Idealist**

   The negotiator plans for tomorrow. He/She is future oriented. He/She is only interested in constructing today for a better world tomorrow. He/She is over-enthusiastic about grand designs and "wild" projects.

---

[1] Ichazo, Oscar. *The Human Process for Enlightenment and Freedom.* New York: Arica Institute. Copyright 1976, pp. 60-63. Used with permission.

8. Over-Just

The negotiator is mainly concerned with fairness and justice. He/She wants to make sure that any decision or agreement is fair to all parties involved in the negotiation.

9. Over-Non-Conformist

The negotiator does not agree with the conventional rules of social interactions and negotiations. He/She is ready to try new behavior, new ways to communicate.

6. Readings

1. Hermann, S.M., and Korenich, M. *Authentic Management: A Gestalt Orientation to Organizations and their Development.* Reading, MA: Addison-Wesley, 1977.

2. Perls, F. *Gestalt Therapy Verbatim.* Moab, UT: Real People Press, 1969.

3. Zinker, J. *Creative Process in Gestalt Therapy.* New York: Vintage Books, 1978.

CHAPTER 9
Negotiations Across Cultures

"The mental maps that we carry with us, based as they are on our own cultural experience, are little better than those Columbus had when he sailed West to find India in 1492. There are even great continents yet to be discovered — vast areas of human experience about which Western man knows nothing."

Edward T. Hall

Negotiating across cultures is what intercultural negotiations are all about. It is easy to negotiate and communicate when we meet with someone we know. We can plan all our tactics and strategies in advance with a fairly accurate forecast of the results we can expect to achieve. But it is different when our "opponent" is from another culture. The mental map is not a reliable guide any more. We have to program ourselves afresh and learn about people from previously unknown cultures, the patterns of their social interaction, their values and beliefs.

There are at least five assumptions we have to bear in mind concerning negotiations across cultures:

1. Planning is critical. We should know sufficiently, if not intimately, about the culture of people we are going to negotiate with. Then we have to carefully plan our moves. There are some things that are going to work as irritants. We should try to avoid them. There are other things which are likely to facilitate the process. We should use them in an effective way.

2. Cultural stereotypes are misleading in the sense that no two human beings belonging to the same culture are going to respond to reality in exactly the same way. So while we can follow a particular approach to negotiation with another culture, we should be prepared to show sufficient flexibility if things do not work out well for us. The only law which governs intercultural negotiations is that there is no law.

3. Language is an important link across cultures and between people. But it is also a barrier. Words have different meanings. The perception of reality is not always the same. Therefore, to be effective negotiators, we should check understanding from time to time, keep a slow pace, and make liberal use of questions.

4. Non-verbal communication is a most significant factor in the intercultural negotiations. What we cannot convey through words, we convey through our gestures and body movements. And what we convey through

words is sometimes negated by our physical expressions. Since there is no universal guide to the language of silence, we have to be extremely careful about the meanings we convey, consciously or unconsciously.

5. Trust in the goodness of human nature is vital. Mutual mistrust and suspicion lead to feelings of contempt and hinder the communication process. And without communication, there is no negotiation.

Workshop 9

1. Aim: To enhance the overall intercultural negotiating capacity of the participants.

2. Objective: Participants will:

(1) Analyze various critical factors in intercultural negotiations;

(2) Compare some of the key cultural traits in order to plan their negotiations; and

(3) Examine the cultural profiles of some selected negotiators.

3. Process:

First Exercise. **PHASE 1.** The group is asked to analyze the General Semantics Model given below and relate it to intercultural negotiations.

General Semantics Model[1]

Some Applications	Some Suggestions
1. No two things are identical.	1. Try to use descriptive terms rather than ones that express approval or disapproval.
2. No one thing stays the same.	2. Try to use phrases that indicate conditions that should be considered with a statement ("in our culture" or "from our point of view," etc.)
3. It is not possible to tell all about anything.	3. Try to move in the direction of substituting precise words for vague ones.
4. The same word may be used to represent different "realities," while similar events or experiences are sometimes called by different names.	4. Try to become more alert to the ways in which cultural conditioning shapes our value judgments.
5. Statements of opinion are often confused with statements of fact.	5. Try to recognize the degree to which the mind itself projects the kinds of answers that it obtains.
	6. Try to avoid either-or evaluations, substituting instead the idea of a continuum which encourages answers expressed by "in-between" amounts when appropriate.
	7. Try to become more suspicious of our own "wisdom."

PHASE 2. A list of five stereotypical cultural (value) orientations related to the "white" and "blue" cultures, given below, is presented to the group. Participants are asked to analyze their impact on negotiations between these two cultures.

---

[1]Based on Seymour Fersh "Semantics and the Study of Cultures," *Learning About Peoples and Cultures,* Seymour Fersh, ed., Evanston, IL: McDougal, Littel & Co., 1979, pp. 87-91.

White and Blue Cultures

Some Key Cultural Orientations

White Culture	Blue Culture
1. Religion encompasses all aspects of life.	1. Religion is a matter of personal choice and does not have any significant impact on one's working life.
2. Work progresses at a very slow pace.	2. Hard work and keeping deadlines are two assumptions central to this culture.
3. Small talk is part of business negotiations.	3. Business negotiations are a serious affair with no small talk or humor.
4. Time is important but is not well-organized. Being late is normal.	4. Time scheduling is extremely important. Punctuality is maintained.
5. Generous hospitality precedes business meetings (negotiations).	5. Meetings are businesslike; few amenities are provided.

PHASE 3. Participants are divided into three teams and each team is provided with a set of perceptions about Americans as others see them.[2] The teams are not aware of the fact that they have been provided with different sets of perceptions. The task assigned to each team is to come up with a set of guidelines on "how to negotiate with Americans."

Team A: Americans are (as seen by other people):

    A. *CARELESS:* with dress, possessions, rules, manners, ceremonies, nature, relationships, political dealings with lesser nations.

    B. *SELF-INDULGENT:* pursuing only material happiness.

    C. *COMPLACENT yet ARROGANT:* peculiarly ethnocentric, to the point of embarrassment; misunderstand "honor."

    D. *COLONISTIC:* ethnocentrically imperialistic; have disregard for other systems; overly proud of own self.

Team B: Americans are (as seen by other people):

    A. *SENTIMENTAL, ROMANTIC:* prone to extremes in emotional expressions; too open, e.g., "movies."

---

[2]American characteristics selected from Tyler, V. Lynn, et. al. *Reading Between the Lines,* Provo, UT: Eyring Research Institute, 1978, part A-2.

B. *MATERIALISTIC:* usually honest; ambitious, with success seeming paramount; vastness and bigness appear to be more desirable than appropriateness.

C. *SELF-INDULGENT:* sometimes very brash, yet demand possibly too much of selves and others.

D. *COMPETITIVE yet EQUALITARIAN:* (a paradox to most non-Americans) no real aristocracy, class, or rank; what is achieved or held seems temporary.

E. *INDEPENDENT and DIFFERENT:* individual feelings not able to fit any mold; fiercely defensive if seemingly offended or encroached upon.

Team C: Americans are (as seen by other people);

A. *GENEROUS/HOSPITABLE:* as victors in war, as friends in need, as UN benefactors, as neighbors.

B. *RESOURCEFUL:* lovers of common sense and results; inventions, innovations, and flexibility; they are NOW-oriented — though the future is considered worth sacrificing for.

After the three teams have made their presentations, the trainer will highlight the following issues:

— We should be careful about *stereotyped* views of nationalities.

— No two persons are exactly the same in any given society.

— The best way to respond to another culture is to be empathetic. Showing active concern for other people helps.

PHASE 4. Participants meet in threes. Five critical incidents that have been previously taped are presented to them one by one. The tape for each incident will be played twice so that participants fully understand the situation. Five minutes are allowed for discussion and agreement on a single best response in each situation. Each time the groups make their presentations, the trainer will try to identify their *negotiating styles* and *modes of negotiating.*

Critical Incidents

1. You have been sent by your organization to work on a development project in a third world country. You decide to adapt a participative style of leadership with a strong people orientation. In all official meetings you encourage the local supervisors to participate in decisions, but you find that they invariably look to you for all important decisions and shy away from any deeper involvement. Soon you discover that the work on the project is behind schedule and most of the controls are ineffective. You come to the conclusion that "locals" are too lazy and do not want to invest their energies in the project. You decide to convene a meeting of the supervisory staff to

share your perceptions, but you are shocked to hear the comment of your senior supervisor who tells you that the project was suffering due to ineffective leadership. All members of the group seem to concur with this view. How do you negotiate commitment of the staff to the project without conceding the point that your leadership style was ineffective? You are required to make a very brief, but highly effective statement to uphold your position.

2. As a senior diplomat of your country at your embassy in Jamira, you are leading a delegation to negotiate with the local government asking for liberalization in the import policy of that country in line with liberalized imports permitted by your own country. It seems that you are not achieving much success. The leader of the Jamira delegation makes a long statement that upsets you and your colleagues and you wish to make an effective response. The statement of Jamira's leader in summary form may be said to contain five major points:

(1) We are a proud sovereign nation and we do not wish to delegate domestic policy formulation to alien powers.

(2) Government policies reflect the political ideology of the party in power.

(3) Import-export policies in general reflect the principles enshrined in the doctrine of comparative advantage.

(4) Our imports are showing an increasing trend and no other country has ever complained of Jamira following restrictive trade policies.

(5) Our government does not encourage import of substandard industrial products.

What do you say?

3. You are a teacher in Kabul. The son of your principal is attending Habibia, the most prestigious high school in the country, and the son of the principal of Habibia is attending your school and is, in fact, in your class. He is a poor student and it is obvious to you and his classmates that he is failing English miserably. You have consistently warned the class that you will pass only those who know their English and will show no favoritism in grades. Most of the students gradually have come to believe this and are finally working hard. There has been, you have noticed, less cheating on homework and quizzes, and you considered this a good indication that they have finally begun to see the worth of individual achievement.

One day your principal comes to you and asks you to pass Habibia principal's son, since the principal of Habibia is doing a similar favor for his son there. You want to continue your good working relationship with your principal and yet you do not want to betray your own values. How will you "negotiate" the situation? (Prepared by Rosalind Pearson and Janet Bing, Peace Corps).

4. As a young tourist in France, you have been invited to dinner at the home of a French business associate of your father. You know that under such circumstances it is considered polite to bring a bouquet of flowers to the hostess. Accordingly, you arrive at the door of the apartment with a handsome bouquet of white chrysanthemums. As your hostess greets you, you offer the bouquet to her. You notice a look of surprise and distaste cross her face. You are at a loss to know why she is hesitant to accept the bouquet. What do you tell her? (Prepared by Genelle Morain).

5. You are a senior manager in a large multinational corporation. Normally you get along very well with your deputy but you are often irritated by his habit of lowering his eyes every time you talk to him. One day you decide to have a "little" talk with him, but as soon as you start speaking he lowers his head and looks down at the floor. What do you say?

Second Exercise. Participants analyze the following imaginary negotiation simulation (see Conceptual Framework: Input 2 for the debriefing of the exercise).

BELIZE: A SCENARIO OF THE CLASH OF CULTURES[3]

1987 will long be remembered as the year the United States learned the hard way about intercultural negotiation. The tensions stemming from her mishandling of the "Belize Crisis" finally forced her to wake up and open her eyes and mind to the value of intercultural empathy.

Oddly enough, the entire episode began in one of Latin America's smallest and newest countries. Belize had recently gained independence in the late 1970s after many years spent under the protection of the United Kingdom. As British Honduras, her borders and sovereignty had been constantly challenged by her neighbors; Mexico to the north and particularly Guatemala to the west and south. These border tensions continued to fester long past her independence, culminating in mid-1987 over the question of whether or not the U.K. was exercising undue control over the upcoming Belize elections scheduled for June 1 of that year. Speculation centered on Britain's supposed interest in mineral deposits long claimed to be hidden in Belize's northern regions. Discord and anger built up between Guatemala and the U.K. over these questions, with the United States a very interested bystander, until the kettle reached a boiling point in early May.

Taken from *The Isolated Years: America's Search for Herself* Chapter 6 "Belize: A Clash of Cultures" by Arthur Schlesinger III (Praeger Publ., Toronto) 1990.

---

[3]Created by Bonnie E. Wetterer, Washington, D.C., 1982. Based on a course taught by P. Casse at Georgetown University.

Taken from the diary of an unknown Guatemalan soldier found after the Battle of Orange Walk.

Looking back on the "Belize Crisis," as we at the State Department dubbed the Latin American troubles of 1987, I would pinpoint May 16 as the first day of importance for us. On that day, Guatemala formally protested to the United Nations concerning the upcoming elections in Belize. Guatemalan president, Fernando Rios argued, in a very controversial statement read by his envoy that Britain was attempting to control Belize election campaigning and alleged that the U.K. hoped to rig the outcome so as to benefit from Belize's alleged mineral resources. This was by no means the first UN statement to create a hubbub in the State Department but it was certainly one of the most sensitive. How could we maintain good relations with Guatemala and the rest of Latin American when our oldest, closest ally was being put on 'trial' by her accusers? This was a difficult issue. I am afraid we did not handle it well.

Taken from *MEMOIRS: The Story of U.S. Diplomacy 1985-1988* by Jeanne Kirkpatrick, former Secretary of State. New York: Alfred Knopf, 1989.

The London Times: May 18, 1987

CLARENDON DENIES OVERT BELIZE INVOLVEMENT BY UK

The Washington Post: May 19, 1987

UK UNDER PRESSURE ADMITS BELIZE AID

Le Monde: May 20, 1987

Clarendon dit:

NOUS RESTERONS EN BELIZE JUSQUE AUX ELECTIONS

The Belize Times: May 25, 1987

JUNE 1 ELECTIONS ON: PRESSURES BETWEEN GUATEMALA AND BRITAIN BUILD

As the troubles between my country and Great Britain grew, I knew that the chances for peaceful settlement were slim. Clarendon, Great Britain's Prime Minister, and the rest of his government refused to understand the way things work in our part of the world: independence, integrity, dignity of the individual, spirituality — all are values that we cherish. Yet Britain, in her single-minded pursuit of what she deemed "freedom," failed to see that her ideas and values were not ours. Negotiations, carried on at the behest of the United States, gave further evidence of this lack of caring or understanding of our values. The North American delegation and their European brothers filled the air with cries of "let's get down to business"; "let's cement an agreement"; "let's deal with the mineral rights in a business-like way." They refused to slow down and accept the way things are and must be. If there are indeed minerals in the poor country of Belize then that is the way God meant it to be. How could we trust these capitalists who claimed to have the best interests of Belize at heart? Fifty years ago we might have bowed to their wishes but not today.

Taken from *Days of Glory: Latin America Comes of Age* by Fernando Rios, former President of Guatemala.

The Belize Billboard: June 2, 1987

ELECTIONS HELD UK FACTIONS WIN

The New York Times: June 3, 1987

UK, GUATEMALA TENSIONS WORSEN
US-LED TALKS TO CONTINUE

Time Magazine: June 4, 1987

KIRKPATRICK SAYS: "WE WILL REMAIN NEUTRAL"

The Washington Post: June 5, 1987

KIRKPATRICK SHUTTLE DIPLOMACY FAILS
BELIZE CRISIS AT HAND

One of the luxuries of a retired statesman is the opportunity to see and comment freely upon international and domestic crises without fear of jeopardizing one's own position. It is a special luxury when one has already been involved in a similar situation and can offer thoughts drawing from that experience. Such was my position during the Belize crisis.

Most obviously, the Latin Americans are devils to deal with. They are slow to work but quick to anger and emotion. They deal not in useful, concrete, here-and-now propositions but offer up vague, futuristic, often childishly trusting goals, sometimes not even relevant to the problem at hand. They can be incompetent, inexperienced diplomats having long outlived their usefulness but remaining strictly for glory's sake. Accordingly, I was very frustrated when I attempted shuttle diplomacy during the Falklands crisis. And, the Belize Crisis was much the same for my successor. Latin America's leaders just would not listen to reason. The United States was destined to get bruised, as she had in 1982.

Taken from *Toppled Governments* by Alexander Haig, former Secretary of State. Boston: Houghton-Mifflin, 1990.

I hated dealing with the Americans and British. First of all, their motives for stirring up trouble in our part of the world were highly suspect, to say the least. Money, or the anticipation of it, undoubtedly spurred them on. Secondly, trying to negotiate with their diplomats was a nightmare. They consistently refused to stand back and survey the entire picture. Did they not realize that the Belize Crisis and what it involved would (and did) largely determine U.S.-Latin American relations in the coming years? Much broader, deeper issues than the elections or mineral rights were being decided — yet they consistently forced the negotiations into a rigid, timed framework. Nothing could flower in the straight-jacket they placed upon us. And nothing did.

Taken from *As We Saw It: The Belize Crisis of 1987* by Jose Aquila-Bosch, Guatemalan Foreign Minister. Panama City: Universidad Press, Panama City: 1992.

The London Times: June 9, 1987

GUATEMALA INVADES BELIZE — CLARENDON DISPATCHES FLEET

When reports arrived of the Guatemalan invasion, we were faced with one of the most important decisions of my tenure as Secretary of State. Obviously, the U.S. could not condone such irresponsible behavior. International law was not being respected and as world leaders, we had to do something. Furthermore, being honest, I must admit that the Rios government's personal irresponsibility frustrated all my concentrated efforts at shuttle diplomacy. Knowing full well the time limits pressing upon us, Rios insisted on dwelling upon the most insignificant topics. While I attempted to shift our conversation to the important matters at hand, the Guatemalan diplomats could not confine themselves and talked of ideals and goals that had nothing to do with what we needed to discuss. Consequently, as the election date bore down upon us, I realized invasion was imminent. When the confirmation of my fears appeared, I was happy to support the British. It was not until much later that I realized what damage I had done by not really listening to what the Guatemalans had been talking about. It was a difficult and costly lesson to learn.

Taken from *MEMOIRS . . .* by Jeanne Kirkpatrick

As June 11 dawned, the world continued to focus its angry eye upon the United States. Why had she not done something; taken some action; succeeded at negotiating? European allies maintained Clarendon's supreme right to send in the British fleet to deal swiftly, without talk, with the renegade Latin Americans. Guatemala's South American counterparts talked of dignity, the right to international respect, and, occasionally, even mentioned spirituality. Kirkpatrick and her advisors surrounded themselves with reams of paper on related topics and discussed the feasibility of each projected American position. A decision came soon.

Taken from *The Isolated Years . . .* by Arthur Schlesinger III

The International Herald Tribune: June 14, 1987

US TO SIDE WITH UK ON BELIZE INVASION

The Los Angeles Times: June 15, 1987

US ALLIES WITH UK ON BELIZE — WHITE HOUSE SAYS 'NO TROOPS'

My first reaction upon hearing the U.S. decision was one of complete, utter, violent anger. The dispatch we subsequently sent to the White House was emotion-filled; pleading; begging them to try and understand what they were doing to the people of Guatemala, of Belize and to their future relations with Latin America. One might believe that the Falklands crisis would have taught them a valuable lesson: Do not declare neutrality and then take sides. But no. My people were forced once again to deal with the money-hungry, power-hungry, unfeeling leaders of the United States. Had Mrs. Kirkpatrick and the others left us to our methods, we might have solved this crisis peacefully. As slow as we are; as contemplative as we seem, it is all for good reason.

Taken from *Days of Glory* by Fernando Rios

The Guatemalan Express: July 1, 1987

CLARENDON CLAIMS UK VICTORY AT HAND — RIOS GOVERNMENT SAYS 'IMPOSSIBLE'

The Washington Post: July 2, 1987

UK VICTORY IN BELIZE EXPECTED SOON, SAYS WHITE HOUSE

The London Times: July 4, 1987

UK WINS IN BELIZE — RIOS CONCEDES DEFEAT

Third Exercise. **PHASE 1.** Participants meet in threes (four to six groups) and answer the following question:

"According to you, what are the main negotiating strategies used by the following cultures: The U.S.A., Japan, Brazil, and Eqypt?"

The teams are encouraged to use *stereotypes* to answer the question as well as the matrix below:

Cultures and Negotiating Strategies				
		Cultures		
Strategies	USA	Japan	Brazil	Egypt
1. Use of power				
2. Courtesy				
3. Withdrawal				
4. 'Divide to Conquer'				
5. Mediation by a third party				
6. Direct negotiation				
7. Ready to lose today in order to win tomorrow				
8. Postpone (freeze on negotiation)				
9. Diplomatic approach				
10. Arbitration				

PHASE 2. The following statements are checked by the group:

Japanese Negotiation	True	False
1. Japanese are extremely concerned about losing face.		
2. Japanese are sensitive to rank.		
3. Japanese value humor above all.		
4. Japanese are vague when they do not have the proper answer to a question.		
5. Japanese are skillful at using others' strengths to win.		

Latin American Negotiation	True	False
1. Latin Americans are conservative and believe in the values of the past.		
2. Latin Americans value personal pride.		
3. Latin Americans enjoy competition.		
4. Latin Americans like to gamble.		
5. Latin Americans are formal.		

French Negotiation	True	False
1. French believe in procedures.		
2. French are imaginative when negotiating.		
3. French like to be liked.		
4. French are status-conscious.		
5. French appreciate logic.		

U.S.A. Negotiation	True	False
1. Americans are informal.		
2. Americans rely on experts when they negotiate.		
3. Americans believe in action.		
4. Americans value "winners."		
5. Americans want quick results.		

Middle East Negotiation	True	False
1. Arabs believe in power.		
2. Arabs are sensitive to eloquence.		
3. Arabs enjoy bargaining for the sake of bargaining.		
4. Arabs are religious.		
5. Arabs believe in etiquette.		

4. Time: One full day.

5. Conceptual Framework:

INPUT 1

Seven Approaches to Saying "No"[4]

In Turkey "no" is signaled by moving one's head backwards while rolling one's eyes upwards. However, to an American this movement is close to the signal used for saying "yes." Further, in still other cultures, head shaking may have nothing to do with affirmation or negation. In parts of India, rolling the head slowly from side to side means something like "yes, go on. I am listening . . ."

It is not hard to find examples of similar ways of expressing "no" relations across several cultures. These are worth listing.

---

[4]From Rubin, J. "How To Tell When Someone Is Saying No." *Topics in Culture Learning,* Vol. 4. Honolulu HI: East West Center, East-West Culture Learning Institute, August 1976, pp. 61-63.

1. Be silent, hesitate, show a lack of enthusiasm. In many cultures in the world, being silent is a way of refusing an offer or an invitation or of giving an answer.

2. Offer an alternative. In some cases in order not to offend or to direct the conversation away from the request, the addressee may divert attention by suggesting an alternative.

3. Postponement (delaying answers). Often in response to a request to perform something or to an invitation, "no" is indicated by postponement.

4. Put the blame on a third party on something over which you have no control.

5. Avoidance. One way to answer a question or an offer is to avoid responding directly.

6. General acceptance of an offer but giving no details.

7. Divert and distract the addressee (questioning the question.)

Many of the above seven approaches to saying "no" are found in every culture. A foreigner has trouble when the relations between form and meaning are not the same in two different cultures. For example:

1. Silence may mean "no" in one culture, but "maybe" in another. In the U.S. if you do not receive an answer to an inquiry, it means "no." However, in Britain it means "maybe" or "I'll write later when I have something to say."

2. Verbal cues may give one message but non-verbal cues another.

3. Societies differ in how food is offered and accepted and rejected.

4. In France, when offered something, the best refusal is to say "merci" with a right movement of the head. The translation of this word is "thanks," but it means "no thanks." In the U.S. "thanks" means "yes, thanks."

One of the more interesting observations about "no" is that sometimes "no" may mean "maybe," given the right time and circumstances.

INPUT 2[5]

First of all, the basic problem lay in the shuttle diplomacy/negotiations run by the U.S. State Department. Unfortunately, rather than gently easing the tensions, Kirkpatrick and the rest of the U.S. diplomatic convoy exacerbated them. Each side viewed the negotiations differently. (Note that this analysis can apply to most U.S.-Latin America negotiations.) Guatemala, for example, saw in the shuttle diplomacy a chance to air her grievances and

---

[5]Written by Ms. Bonnie E. Wetterer.

discuss the more idealistic problems at hand. She was not willing to be limited by the type of time and subject restraints which might frustrate deep discussions and patriotic appeals. The U.S., on the other hand, wanted to ram her goals/objectives through the delegations and announce a cease-fire as soon as possible. She desired a factual, analytical, swift, objective, and conclusive discussion of the Belize problem. Her value system dictated that negotiations follow this course.

The Problem: Neither partner was willing to really hear, through culturally-attuned ears, what the other was saying. Both had singular objectives in mind and neither was innovative, flexible, or open — three prerequisites for successful intercultural communication and negotiation.

In the case of the Belize Crisis, such openness was particularly hard to attain. There was indeed a deadline, the June 1 elections, as the U.S. insisted, as well as the potential violation of international law. But there was also an important moral issue, as Guatemala termed the Latin American search for independence and integrity. Both cultures had the right ideas but neither was willing to give.

Apart from these differences concerning the overall issues, cultural idiosyncracies were seen in the negotiating styles of both cultures. Guatemala seemed much more intent on using the talks as a forum to discuss idealistic, futuristic ideas. She cared little about the time involved, seeing the issues as too important to be hemmed in. Furthermore, to please the Americans, the Guatemalans would often make non-committal, innocuous statements that seemed to be in agreement with the U.S. stance but were really only rhetoric.

On the American side, business, time, and money, not people or the deeper moral issues held sway. All the Kirkpatrick delegation interested itself in was victory at the bargaining table, no matter how shallow. In contrast to the Guatemalans, the U.S. delegation eagerly and unwisely lived up to their reputation as money-hungry, showy imperialsts.

Having laid out the situation — two cultures with very different goals and objectives — what could have been done to facilitate agreement on the issue of Belize? It could be argued that three principles should govern all international/intercultural negotiations between Latin America and the U.S.:

1. The *common history* and the *close proximity* of these neighbors should be kept in the heart and on the minds of everyone at the negotiating table. Latin Americans and North Americans share a common European heritage as well as a history of seeking freedom through revolution. The two groups also mingle in terms of exports, religion, and immigrants as well as through American programs such as the Alliance for Progress. Finally, the mere geographical proximity and the consequent interest in maintaining good relations adds another element of closeness to the two cultures. By constantly stressing these common factors, it will be much easier to lessen the differences and search for agreements.

2. While keeping in mind what we have in common, each partner should also *attune* his *hearing* and thinking to the cultural differences of negotiating style between Latin America and North America. Obviously, from the example of the "Belize Crisis," one can see that Latin Americans are less hasty and more interested in the people-oriented aspects of the discussion. North Americans, however, tend to be hurried, goal-oriented, and less personal. Each negotiating partner should keep these differences in mind and learn to compensate for them. Let the Latin American teams insert their thoughts on the deep moral question involved. And, bend a little on the North American's insistence on punctuality. Each side will be happier and, again, the common ground for negotiation will be firmer.

3. Finally, *communicate*. Although this principle sounds the easiest to implement, in reality, it is the most difficult. Both the Latin American and the North American negotiating partners must express their thoughts and goals clearly and objectively. Furthermore, each group must learn to put these ideas in terms that make sense to the other partner. In other words, both partners must adjust their ideas to the cultural limitations and goals of the other and communicate, unambiguously, these ideas. Only when these bargaining points are communicated *across* the intercultural barrier can any negotiating begin. As it progresses, basic negotiating premises will be established by both sides and, thanks to the building of common ground, can be dealt with imaginatively and sanely.

When this happens, the negotiating process can and will be successful. Two cultures will be able to mix and produce compromises and solid results. Leaders from both countries will be able to blend factual and intuitive approaches creatively, benefiting each side.

INPUT 3

Cultural Approaches to Negotiation

Portrait of an American Negotiator[6]

A successful American Negotiator is someone who:

1. Knows when to compromise;

2. Takes a firm stand at the beginning of the negotiation;

3. Refuses to make concessions beforehand;

4. Keeps his/her cards close to his/her chest;

5. Accepts compromises only when the negotiation is deadlocked;

6. Sets up the general principles and delegates the detail work to associates;

---

[6]Inspired by Cannon, L. "Fresh Tests Awaiting Negotiator-In-Chief." *The Washington Post,* Monday, March 28, 1983.

7. Keeps a maximum of options open before negotiation;

8. Operates in good faith;

9. Respects the "opponents;"

10. States his/her position as clearly as possible;

11. Knows when he/she wishes a negotiation to move on;

12. Is fully briefed about the negotiated issues;

13. Has a good sense of timing and is consistent;

14. Makes the other party reveal his or her position while keeping his/her own position hidden as long as possible;

15. Lets the other negotiator come forward first and looks for the best deal.

Portrait of an Indian Negotiator[7]

Gandhi called his approach to negotiation *SATYAGRAHA*, which means "firmness in a good cause," and combines strength with the love of truth. A successful negotiator is someone who:

1. Looks for and says the truth;

2. Is not afraid of speaking up and has no fears;

3. Exercises self-control ("the weapons of the *SATYAGRAHA* are within him")'

4. Seeks solutions that will please all the parties involved ("*SATYA-GRAHA* aims to exalt both sides");

5. Respects the other party ("the opponent must be weaned from error by patience and sympathy. Weaned, not crushed; converted not annihilated");

6. Does not use violence or insults;

7. Is ready to change his/her mind and differ with himself or herself at the risk of being seen as inconsistent and unpredictable;

8. Puts things into perspective and switches easily from the small picture to the big one;

9. Is humble and trusts the opponent;

10. Is able to withdraw, use silence, and learn from within;

---

[7]Inspired by Fischer, L. "Satyagraha" from *The Life of Mahatma Ghandi* New York: Harper, 1950 and Fischer, L. (Ed.), *The Essential Ghandi* New York: Random House, Inc. 1962.

11. Relies on himself or herself, his/her own resources and strengths;

12. Appeals to the other party's spiritual identity ("to communicate, the West moves or talks. The East sits, contemplates, suffers");

13. Is tenacious, patient, and persistent;

14. Learns from the opponent and avoids the use of secrets;

15. Goes beyond logical reasoning and trusts his/her instinct as well as faith.

Portrait of an Arab Negotiator[8]

Those Arabs who are Moslem and are involved in negotiation believe in using the traditional way to settle disputes, namely, to use *mediators.* a successful mediator is someone who:

1. Protects all the parties' honor, self-respect, and dignity;

2. Avoids direct confrontations between opponents;

3. Is respected and trusted by all;

4. Does not put the parties involved in a situation where they have to show weakness or admit defeat;

5. Has the necessary prestige to be listened to;

6. Is creative enough to come up with honorable solutions for all parties;

7. Is impartial and can understand the positions of the various parties without leaning toward one or the other;

8. Is able to resist any kind of pressure that the opponents could try to exercise on him ("In sum, the ideal mediator is a man who is in a position, because of his personality, status, respect, wealth, influence, and so on to create in the litigants the desire to conform with his wishes");

9. Uses references to people who are highly respected by the opponents to persuade them to change their minds on some issues ("do it *for the sake* of your father");

10. Can keep secrets and in so doing gains the confidence of the negotiating parties;

11. Controls his temper and emotions (or loses it when and where necessary);

12. Can use *conferences* as mediating devices;

13. Knows that the opponents will have problems in carrying out the decisions made during the negotiation;

---

[8]Raphael Patai, excerpt from *The Arab Mind.* Copyright © 1973, 1976, 1983 by Raphael Patai. Reprinted with permission of Charles Scribner's Sons.

14. Is able to cope with the Arab disregard for time;

15. Understands the impact of Islam on the opponents who believe that they possess the truth, follow the Right Path and are going to "win" because their cause is just.

Portrait of a Swedish Negotiator[9]

Swedish negotiators are sometimes perceived by other people as being:

1. Very quiet and thoughtful;

2. Punctual (concerned with time);

3. Extremely polite;

4. Straightforward (they get straight down to business);

5. Eager to be productive and efficient;

6. Heavy-going;

7. Down-to-earth and over-cautious;

8. Rather flexible;

9. Able to and quite good at holding emotions and feelings;

10. Slow at reacting to new (unexpected) proposals;

11. Informal and familiar;

12. Conceited;

13. Perfectionist;

14. Afraid of confrontations;

15. Very private.

Portrait of an Italian Negotiator[10]

Italians define a successful negotiator as someone who:

1. Has a sense of drama (acting is a main part of the culture);

2. Does not hide his or her emotions (which are partly sincere and partly feigned);

3. Reads facial expressions and gestures very well;

4. Has a feeling for history;

---

[9]Phillips-Martinsson, J. *Swedes as Others See Them.* Lund: Utbildningshuset/Studentlitteratur, 1982.

[10]Luigi Barzini, excerpt from *The Italians.* Copyright © 1964 by Luigi Barzini. Reprinted with permission of Atheneum Publishers.

5. Does not trust anybody;

6. Is concerned about the *"bella figura"* or the good impression he or she can create among those who watch his or her behavior;

7. Believes in the individual's initiatives, not so much in teamwork;

8. Is good at being obliging and *"simpatico"* at all times;

9. Is always on the *"qui vive."*

10. Never embraces definite opinions;

11. Is able to come up with new ways to immobilize and eventually destroy his or her opponents;

12. Handles confrontations of power with subtlety and tact;

13. Has a flair for intrigue;

14. Knows how to use flattery;

15. Can involve other negotiators in complex combinations.

6. Readings

1. Brislin, R. W. *Cross-Cultural Encounters.* New York: Pergamon Press, 1981.

2. Harris, P. R., Moran, R. T. *Managing Cultural Differences.* Houston, TX: Gulf Publishing Co., 1979.

3. Launay, R. *La Negociation.* Paris: Editions ESP — Entreprise Moderne d'Editions, 1983.

CHAPTER 10
Negotiation Case Studies

"Formal logic does not fit with reality, because despite the fact that it establishes the principles of logical thinking, it doesn't solve its inherent contradictions with the constant movement of the external world. There are two aspects: You think, and it is as though you have paralyzed everything. Reality doesn't happen that way. In reality everthing flows. This means that your reason is not matching reality."

O. Ichazo

In this final chapter, we present three negotiation case studies and critical incidents. Readers are asked to apply as much as possible of what they have acquired through the reading of the book to a series of real life situations. In a way, we offer them an opportunity to *"test themselves."* Trainers can also look at the five cases as potential training materials to be used in training seminars and workshops.

The cases deal with the following:

1. Interpersonal negotiation;

2. Negotiation for grants;

3. Negotiation in politics.

Workshop 10

1. **Aim:** To provide an opportunity to the readers to apply what they have learned in reading the book to a set of selected negotiating situations.

2. **Objectives:** Participants will:

(1) Try out some of the basis ideas presented in the book;

(2) Determine ways to apply some of the models presented in the book on various situations;

(3) Examine the possiblity of using the case studies as training materials for intercultural negotiation seminars or workshops.

3. Process:

First Exercise

Interpersonal Negotiation

Look at the picture below and assume that the father is trying to persuade his son to go to college, then:

1. Invent a dialogue between the father and his son;

2. Analyze the dialogue you have just created using as much material contained in the book as possible.

Second Exercise

Negotiation for Grants

Assume that you belong to an educational institution and that you have decided to apply for a grant to the foundation described below (see guidelines for grant applications). How would you approach it so as to maximize your chances of getting the money that you need?

Guidelines for Grant Applications

The mission of the multicultural Education Foundation is to support improvements in the quality of education. For the most part, that purpose is realized by grants to institutions of higher learning.

Our support of education takes several forms, and different Foundation programs operate on different bases.

Under our Pre-College Education Program and our Sustaining Program, application for funding is by Foundation invitation. Our incentive program for Individual Aid to Education represents another mode of activity matching the gifts of employees and annuitants of the Foundation and certain of its affiliates to colleges and universities.

In our two other program areas, Education Research and Development and Economics and Management of Higher Education, initiative to submit proposals to the Foundation is left to the prospective grant recipient. The following information is intended to serve as a guide to those areas and to how our application procedure works.

Program Interests

Through the years, teaching and learning and educational policy and administration have been the main areas of attention for the Foundation. We have now extended the range of our activities while redefining certain areas of special interest.

Designed to encompass grants for the broad spectrum of activities in which educational institutions and organizations engage, the Educational Research and Development program is nevertheless governed by several strong priorities. We are especially interested in projects that cross traditional lines between disciplines, professions, and institutions, and in projects bringing representatives from diverse specializations together to focus on major social issues. We give priority to projects involving re-examination of basic educational purposes, programs, and requirements and to efforts to introduce consideration of values issues into professional and graduate training. We also give preference to projects that reflect a concern for the international dimension of education and the need for heightened awareness of global issues. Under the Economics and Management of Higher Education program, we are interested in projects that will foster improved allocation and use of resources among and within educational institutions and systems, improved understanding of the economic forces affecting educational services and institutions, and improved institutional response to economic change.

While the scope of these two programs is intentionally left broad enough to allow consideration of any proposal concerned with education, grants are ordinarily not made to: (1) support the adoption of established educational or administrative methods or materials, (2) provide funds for capital improvements (equipment, buildings, or endowment), (3) support institutional scholarship funds, or (4) fund those standard course or curriculum development activities normally covered by institutional budgets.

Eligibility

Educational institutions or organizations that are located in the United States, its Territories or possessions and that are qualified for tax exemption under the Internal Revenue Code are eligible for grants. The Foundation does not make grants to individuals.

Application

An institution wishing to submit a proposal, should send the Foundation an outline. There are no specific deadlines; each proposal will be reviewed as it is received.

Proposal Outlines

The following information should be supplied in the indicated order on no more than five typewritten pages. Submit five copies of the outline, but submit no other information unless specifically requested to do so.

(1) Name of the organization; name, title, office address, and telephone number of the Chief Executive Officer.

(2) Name of the head of the unit in which the project is to be conducted.

(3) Name, title, office address, and telephone number of the person to be in charge of the project.

(4) Brief descriptive title of the project.

(5) Total amount of grant request.

(6) A statement of aims of the proposed project and an explanation of the needs or problems to be addressed.

(7) A description of related work by others to solve the above problems and an explanation of how the proposed project expands upon or complements those efforts.

(8) A full and precise description of the proposed project or activity, covering both what is to be done and how it is to be done.

(9) An explanation of how the effectiveness of the project will be measured.

(10) An explanation of which groups will benefit from the project and how the results of the project will be communicated to these groups.

(11) Name, title, and qualifications of each person participating in the project.

(12) A detailed budget, giving a breakdown of project costs and listing separately the amounts to be contributed by the organization/institution, the amounts to be covered by the other funding sources. (Note: The Foundation does not permit allocation of its funds for indirect costs.) If the project is an on-going one, a history of prior funding should be provided.

(13) A statement of the expected duration of the project, and, in the case of long-term projects, an explanation of how the project would be continued upon expiration of the requested grant.

(14) The name, title, and original signature (on one copy) of an individual authorized to commit the organization to participation in the project.

Third Exercise

Negotiation in Politics

A. Situation

The *government* has asked *the representatives of the people, the administrative authorities* and *the experts* in various areas to rank order a list of development areas for negotiating purposes (keeping in mind that resources are limited).

B. Task

Each group (people, administration, experts, government) separately rank order the following items:

(a) hospitals
(b) roads
(c) employment
(d) schools
(e) medical research
(f) social security
(g) old age benefits
(h) universities

(i) agriculture
(j) banking
(k) industries
(l) tourism
(m) railroads
(n) telephone system
(o) water
(p) energy
(q) cultural activities
(r) construction
(s) leisure
(t) new technologies

Process: The representatives of the four groups meet and decide on:

(a) The way the negotiation is going to be conducted;

(b) A joint ranking.

When finished, a discussion follows on the various "cultural" ways (typical of the four target groups represented in the negotiation) to look at the items listed.

4. Time: An average of one hour per case study.

5. Conceptual Framework: See all the former inputs.

Epilogue: Everything is Negotiable

And so negotiation goes on . . . The book is over and it seems that training for negotiation is becoming more and more appealing to many decision-makers from various countries, sectors and organizations.

We would like to conclude with a **story** (see the section of the book on the power of metaphors in negotiation) which will illustrate the importance for a trainer to apply what he or she preaches when running a seminar on negotiation (this at the **conscious level**) and demonstrate something else that we shall say nothing about because it is geared to the **unconscious mind** which knows anyway.

Some time ago, we were invited by the Training Manager of an international organization to design and conduct a two-day workshop on negotiation skills and strategies for a group of twenty-five decision-makers from Third World countries.

So, one evening we met with the group in a resort place selected by the people in charge of the program. It was about 7 o'clock in the evening.

The Training Manager introduced us to the participants and we started by clarifying the objectives and content of the workshop.

We then proceeded with a presentation on two key assumptions related to negotiation, namely that:

— **Negotiation is an on-going process** in the sense that it happens all the time (We negotiate with ourself, with others including our spouses, children, bosses, colleagues, friends, etc.) and is about everything:

— **Everything is negotiable . . .**

Right at that moment, the Training Manager took the floor and said in a low key manner, but quite loud enough so that everybody was able to catch it, "Except that this session will be over by nine o'clock tonight!"

We could not believe it . . .

As matter of fact, we felt quite awful. There we were, at the beginning of a session on negotiation and confronted in an unexpected way with a basic contradiction which had the potential not only to destroy our credibility as experts in negotiation, but also to jeopardize the entire training effort.

Well, it was too late to say anything to the Training Manager and we decided (without consulting each other at least verbally) to proceed with the presentation, being at the same time fully aware that some of the group members had some reservation regarding the relevance of what was going to be covered afterwards.

The interaction with the group went well, although we could feel some tension in the room . . .

At eight thirty sharp, we introduced a highly motivating self-assessment exercise (the one on the four value orientations and their impact on communication and negotiation) to the group. They went through the exercise step-by-step and by nine o'clock, were ready for the de-briefing to learn the significance of their answers in relation to their communication and negotiation styles.

They were ready and . . . waiting . . .

The trainer in charge of that part of the session turned around and said to the group, "I am extremely sorry, but since it is 9 p.m. and the decision has been made to stop at this time of the evening, I am not in a position to give you the keys of the exercise right now. I am afraid it will have to wait until tomorrow morning."

The participants were outraged. They protested in a very forceful way to the trainer who looked at the Training Manager. The latter said:

"All right . . . you can proceed . . . and take the time that you need . . ."

Then the trainer faced the group, smiled and said:

"You see, **everything is negotiable!**"

Pierre Casse   *Surinder Deol*

Washington, D.C.
March 5, 1985